CONTESTING CONQUEST

guzmā.   michvacā.

CONTESTING CONQUEST

Indigenous Perspectives on the Spanish Occupation of Nueva Galicia

Ida Altman

The Pennsylvania State University Press
University Park, Pennsylvania

Library of Congress Cataloging-in-Publication Data

Names: Altman, Ida, author.
Title: Contesting conquest : indigenous perspectives
    on the Spanish occupation of Nueva Galicia / Ida
    Altman.
Other titles: Latin American originals ; 12.
Description: University Park, Pennsylvania :
    The Pennsylvania State University Press, [2017] |
    Series: Latin American originals ; 12 | Includes bib-
    liographical references and index.
Summary: "An English translation of accounts of
    the experiences and responses of the indigenous
    peoples of western Mexico in the first half of the
    sixteenth century to Spanish efforts to establish
    control over the region that they would call Nueva
    Galicia"—Provided by publisher.
Identifiers: LCCN 2017025908 | ISBN 9780271078564
    (pbk. : alk. paper)
Subjects: LCSH: Nueva Galicia—History—16th cen-
    tury—Sources. | Mexico—History—Conquest,
    1519–1540—Sources. | Indians of Mexico—Mex-
    ico—Nueva Galicia—History—16th century—
    Sources. | Indians, Treatment of—Mexico—Nueva
    Galicia—History—16th century—Sources.
    | Spaniards—Mexico—Nueva Galicia—His-
    tory—16th century—Sources. | Mixton War,
    1541–1542—Sources.
Classification: LCC F1296 .A65 2017 | DDC 972/
    .02—dc23
LC record available at https://lccn.loc.gov/2017025908

The Pennsylvania State University Press is a member
of the Association of American University Presses.

It is the policy of The Pennsylvania State University
Press to use acid-free paper. Publications on uncoated
stock satisfy the minimum requirements of Ameri-
can National Standard for Information Sciences—
Permanence of Paper for Printed Library Material,
ANSI Z39.48–1992.

This book is printed on paper that contains 30% post-
consumer waste.

This book is dedicated to the memory of

Richmond F. Brown and James Lockhart.

CONTENTS

ILLUSTRATIONS

Latin American Originals (LAO) is a series of primary-source texts on colonial Latin America. LAO volumes are accessible editions of texts translated into English—most of them for the very first time. Of the twelve volumes now in print, nine illuminate aspects of the Spanish invasions in the Americas during the long century of 1494–1614, and three push our understandings of the spiritual conquest into surprising new territories.

Taken in the chronological order of their primary texts, *Of Cannibals and Kings* (LAO 7) comes first. It presents the earliest written attempts to describe Native American cultures, offering striking insight into how the first Europeans in the Americas struggled from the very start to conceive a New World. *The Native Conquistador* (LAO 10) comes next, telling the story of the famous Spanish conquest expeditions into Mexico and Central America from 1519 to 1524—but through an indigenous perspective, built around an alternative leading protagonist (Ixtlilxochitl, the king of Tetzcoco), written by his great-great-grandson. Viewed through the prism of the Ixtlilxochitl dynasty, the so-called conquest of Mexico looks startlingly different.

Next, chronologically, are LAO 2, 1, and 9. *Invading Guatemala* shows how reading multiple accounts of conquest wars (in this case, Spanish, Nahua, and Maya versions of the Guatemalan conflict of the 1520s) can explode established narratives and suggest a more complex and revealing conquest story. *Invading Colombia* challenges us to view the difficult Spanish invasion of Colombia in the 1530s as more representative of conquest campaigns than the better-known assaults on the Aztec and Inca Empires. It complements *The Improbable Conquest,* which presents letters written between 1537 and 1556 by Spaniards struggling to found a colony along the hopefully named Río de la Plata. Their trials and tribulations make the persistence of the colonists seem improbable indeed.

The present volume, LAO 12, adds intriguingly to that trio. In *Contesting Conquest*, Ida Altman, the leading expert on the Spanish invasions of Nueva Galicia, offers new perspectives on that region's understudied early history. We read of the grim, messy tale of repeated efforts at conquest and colonization from the late 1520s through 1545, but from a surprising angle: our guides through those events are primarily indigenous witnesses and informants, their voices deftly identified, selected, and presented here.

The History of the New World (LAO 11) slots in next, offering the first English translation since 1847 of significant portions of a 1565 Italian book that was a sixteenth-century best seller in five languages. Its author, the merchant-adventurer Girolamo Benzoni, mixed sharp observations and sympathy for indigenous peoples with imaginary tales and wild history, influencing generations of early modern readers and challenging modern readers to sort out fact from fable.

The Conquest on Trial (LAO 3) features a fictional indigenous embassy filing a complaint over the conquest in a court in Spain— the Court of Death. That text, the first theatrical examination of the conquest published in Spain, effectively condensed contemporary debates on colonization into one dramatic package. It contrasts well with *Defending the Conquest* (LAO 4), which presents a spirited, ill-humored, and polemic apologia for the Spanish Conquest, written in 1613 by a lesser-known veteran conquistador.

LAO volumes 5, 6, and 8 all explore aspects of Spanish efforts to implant Christianity in the Americas. *Forgotten Franciscans* casts new light on the spiritual conquest and the conflictive cultural world of the Inquisition in sixteenth-century Mexico. *Gods of the Andes* presents the first English edition of a 1594 manuscript describing Inca religion and the campaign to convert native Andeans. Its Jesuit author is surprisingly sympathetic to preconquest beliefs and practices, viewing them as preparing Andeans for the arrival of the faith from Spain. Both LAO 5 and 6 expose wildly divergent views within the church in Spanish America—both on native religions and on how to replace them with Christianity. Complementing those two volumes by revealing the indigenous side to the same process, *Translated Christianities* presents religious texts translated from Nahuatl and Yucatec Maya. Designed to proselytize and ensure the piety of indigenous parishioners, these texts show how such efforts actually contributed to the development of local Christianities, leading to fascinatingly multifaceted outcomes.

The source texts in LAO volumes are colonial-era rare books or archival documents, written in European or Mesoamerican languages. LAO authors are historians, anthropologists, and scholars of literature who have developed a specialized knowledge that allows them to locate, translate, and present these texts in a way that contributes to scholars' understanding of the period, while also making them readable for students and nonspecialists. Ida Altman does just that, and as one of her generation's most accomplished and respected scholars of both early modern Spain and colonial Mexico, her contributions add particular luster to this series.

—Matthew Restall

ACKNOWLEDGMENTS

I would like to thank Matthew Restall for encouraging me to undertake this project and for his very useful guidance along the way.
Thanks also go to the two anonymous reviewers of the manuscript
for their helpful suggestions, to Susan Silver for her excellent copy-
editing, and to Ellie Goodman for all her help.

Introduction

In August 1521 Hernando Cortés, leading a force of fellow Spaniards, an unknown number of Africans, and a host of indigenous allies from Tlaxcala, a longtime rival of the Mexica, and other provinces, secured the surrender of Tenochtitlan, the Mexica capital of what today is known as the Aztec Empire. After a two-year campaign characterized by its improvisational, stop-and-start quality, Cortés and his men had precipitated the downfall of the dominant political state of central Mexico. Cortés claimed for the Spanish emperor Charles V the greatest prize obtained by any of the thousands of Spaniards who had tried their luck in the territories of the Americas that Christopher Columbus opened to European occupation in 1492. A tale of betrayal, deceit, bravery, and dramatic reversals that took Spaniards into the heart of a startlingly complex, populous, and wealthy civilization rivaling anything they ever had seen or imagined, the story of the conquest of Mexico has fired the popular imagination ever since. Its seemingly definitive conclusion with the fall of Tenochtitlan often is taken to signal the conquest of all of present-day Mexico.[1]

The reality, however, in many senses was far different. Large areas to the north, south, and west of central Mexico, which eventually

1. The scholarly and popular literature on the conquest of central Mexico is extensive. Probably the best-known and most commonly used sources for the Spanish perspective on the conquest are the retrospective history written by Bernal Díaz del Castillo and Hernando Cortés's contemporary letters, both available in translation in multiple editions. Schwartz, *Victors and Vanquished*, includes excerpts from a number of Spanish and indigenous accounts. Fuentes, *Conquistadors*, includes some lesser-known accounts. For a fairly recent interpretation of the conquest, see Restall, *Seven Myths*.

became part of the kingdom of New Spain, remained outside the Spaniards' control and indeed barely contacted by them. Home to a variety of sociopolitical entities and linguistic and ethnic groups, some of these other regions and peoples—the Maya of present-day Yucatan and Guatemala to the south and the diverse peoples of western Mexico—would prove stubbornly resistant to the establishment of Spanish control. The difficult and sometimes prolonged campaigns conducted in these regions outside central Mexico underscore the reality that the surrender of Tenochtitlan and fairly uniform submission of the mostly Nahua peoples of central Mexico were in fact prelude to, rather than the end of, the conquest of Mexico.

For Cortés himself the rewards of conquest also were ambiguous. He received a noble title, Marqués del Valle de Oaxaca, along with extensive lands and grants of *encomienda* that entitled him to exact labor and tribute from thousands of Mexico's native inhabitants. Although the Spanish king and Holy Roman emperor Charles V recognized Cortés as governor, he did not forget that by leading the campaign into the heart of Mexico Cortés had gone well beyond the prerogatives that had been granted to him. While the payoff for the Crown of Cortés's audacity was substantial, Charles V did not intend to institutionalize any individual's defiance of royal authority. Cortés faced progressive limitations on his power as royal officials began to arrive in the new colony, an *audiencia* (high court) was established in 1528, and finally don Antonio de Mendoza was appointed the first viceroy of New Spain in 1535.[2]

Disappointed and frustrated but still driven by enormous ambition, Cortés sponsored an expedition by Cristóbal de Olid in 1522 that resulted in the incorporation of the Tarascan Empire in Michoacan to the west of the central valley of Mexico as a kind of client state under its traditional ruler, the *cazonci*. The following year Spaniards led by Gonzalo de Sandoval moved into Colima, thus providing

2. On Mendoza, Aiton, *Antonio de Mendoza,* is still useful, as is Pérez Bustamante, *Orígenes del gobierno virreinal.* The audiencia established in Mexico City was the second such institution that the Spanish Crown created in the Indies; the first was in Santo Domingo. The audiencia was intended to be the highest governing body for its jurisdiction and combined judicial, executive, and even legislative functions. The first audiencia in Mexico had a president, Nuño de Guzmán, but with the appointment of Mendoza as viceroy of New Spain he assumed that function.

MAP 1 Nueva Galicia in the sixteenth century

Cortés with a foothold on the Pacific coast and access to the South Sea, as Spaniards at that time referred to the Pacific Ocean. He began building shipyards in Zacatula as early as 1523. These activities laid the basis for Cortés's future claims to western Mexico and explorations of the Pacific, bringing him into direct conflict with the man who would become his greatest rival, Nuño de Guzmán. Already serving as governor of Pánuco, a region northeast of central Mexico, Guzmán was appointed president of the first audiencia of Mexico in 1528.[3] Although Guzmán's claims to western Mexico, or Nueva Galicia as it came to be known in the 1530s, prevailed over those of Cortés, in the end both lost out to the authority of the Spanish Crown and its designated representative, the viceroy Mendoza. Charles V was willing to allow men like Cortés and Guzmán to pursue their ambitions as long as they benefited the Crown, but he would not give them free rein over his newly created kingdoms in the distant Americas. Although by comparison to central Mexico the lands and peoples

3. See Chipman, *Nuño de Guzmán.*

of western Mexico might have seemed remote and unimpressive,
asserting viceregal control over them marked a critical step toward
establishing uncontested royal dominion over New Spain.[4]

The territory that Spaniards called Nueva Galicia included much
of what today are the modern Mexican states of Nayarit, Zacatecas,
Aguascalientes, and Jalisco, a vast area of some hundred thousand
square miles stretching from the Pacific coast to the Sierra Madre
Occidental and including much of the plains of north-central Mexico
east to the foothills of the Sierra Madre Oriental. Human settlement
and society there go back millennia. Like other parts of Mesoamerica
the region attracted groups of migrants, probably mainly from the
north. Although doubtless these movements of people at times
entailed conflict and even conquest, for the most part they probably
resulted in a fairly peaceful commingling of groups, fostering mutual
accommodations and considerable diversity in language and lifestyle.
The west is a land of rivers and fertile plains that in at least some areas
supported fairly dense populations of agriculturalists. Rugged mountains and canyons afforded ample hunting as well as mineral wealth.

Nearly everything that is known about western Mexico before
Spanish occupation comes from the archaeological record, although
excavation in the region has been limited compared to the much
more extensive archaeological work that has been conducted in central Mexico or Yucatan. Even so there is strong evidence of sophisti-
cated societies in the west that at one time mined and exported obsid-
ian on a large scale and built monumental structures—the circular
guachimontones located in the state of Jalisco—that were quite distinct from the stepped pyramids found in other parts of Mesoamerica
that are more familiar to us.[5] The earliest reports and accounts produced by Spaniards who entered the region in the 1520s and 1530s
provide a fascinating but incomplete picture of the diverse peoples

4. Colonial-era jurisdictions and nomenclature in what today are modern Mexico
and Central America are somewhat confusing. Technically, western Mexico became
part of the kingdom of Nueva Galicia and thus was distinct from New Spain; it would
acquire its own audiencia, although it was considered a quasi dependency of the audiencia in Mexico City. The kingdom of Guatemala also would have its own audiencia.
All three kingdoms—New Spain, Nueva Galicia, and Guatemala—came under the
authority of the viceroy in Mexico City.
5. For a good overview of archaeological work in the region, see Weigand and
Weigand, *Tenamaxtli y Guaxicar*, and Pollard, "Recent Research."

FIGURE 1 Los Guachimontones, near Teuchitlan (state of Jalisco), dating to 400–700 C.E. Photo courtesy of Phil C. Weigand.

and cultures of the west. Because these accounts were the product of aggressive Spanish campaigns in the region, they depict local societies that already had been affected by the intrusion of hitherto unknown newcomers whose arrival spread destruction and whose expectations placed unprecedented demands on indigenous society.

After securing Michoacan and Colima, Spaniards attempted to move into the rest of western and northwestern Mexico. It took nearly twenty years before they were able to establish unchallenged control over the region.[6] This effort unfolded in three stages. The first of these was the expedition of Francisco Cortés, who led a move into western Mexico on behalf of his much more famous kinsman, Hernando Cortés, in 1524. Probably no more than around twenty-five Spaniards and an unknown number of local people, most likely recruited in Colima, participated in this expedition, which moved north from Colima on the Pacific coast but did not venture beyond

6. For a full treatment of the entire period and the consequences for the indigenous peoples of the west of the Spanish occupation of Nueva Galicia, see Altman, *War for Mexico's West*.

MAP 2 Area contacted by Francisco Cortés

what Spaniards would call the Río Grande de Santiago.[7] This *entrada* (expedition) did not result in a lasting Spanish presence in the region. Although some encomiendas were assigned to Spaniards who were participants, none of them seem to have made much effort to claim the labor and tribute to which the grants entitled them, probably because they would have found themselves too isolated from Spanish society to make good on their ostensible rights. Although the Francisco Cortés expedition often has been portrayed as fairly benign, there is evidence that it entailed conflict and violence, as suggested by the report compiled by two inspectors who were sent by Hernando Cortés in 1525 to visit the region and survey its communities. This account is our earliest source of information on the land and peoples

7. See Sauer, *Colima*, and the interesting study by Romero de Solís, *Conquistador Francisco Cortés*.

of the west. It is clear that they already had experienced disruption from the incursion of the Spaniards, as suggested by statements made by local rulers regarding populations that had retreated or scattered in fear of the newcomers.[8]

The second stage of the Spanish occupation of the west consisted of the much larger, longer, and more aggressive campaign of 1530–31, led by the president of New Spain's audiencia, Nuño de Guzmán. Departing from Mexico City at the end of 1529, Guzmán assembled several hundred Spaniards and thousands of indigenous warriors from central Mexico, a force he subsequently augmented by conscripting thousands of additional native warriors and auxiliaries in Michoacan. The entrada eventually reached as far north as present-day Sinaloa along the Pacific coast. Food supply was a constant challenge as the expedition moved through territory previously unknown to them, and nearly all encounters with local inhabitants resulted in fighting, burning of pueblos, and commandeering of supplies and people to act as the Spaniards' porters. Not only was the campaign highly destructive to local communities, Guzmán's own party suffered enormous losses when a hurricane and flood struck their encampment in September 1530, resulting directly or indirectly in the deaths of perhaps the majority of the Spaniards' Indian allies (*indios amigos*) from drowning, illness, or starvation. Although Guzmán sent for more conscripts from Michoacan and managed to struggle on, his treatment of the *indios amigos* and the native lords who led them, none of whom returned home, occasioned harsh criticism from officials in Mexico City, who began to question Guzmán's conduct of the expedition even before it ended. By the time Guzmán returned south a new audiencia had replaced the first one, and Guzmán was shocked to discover that he had been ousted as president.

The decade that followed Guzmán's campaign of conquest was troubled and disorderly despite Spanish expectations of forging among the varied peoples of the west an *encomendero* society along the lines of what had taken shape in central Mexico.[9] No sooner had

8. "Nuño de Guzmán" includes a reliable and accessible transcription of the 1525 *visitación* (visit of inspection); the original is in expediente 7, legajo 409, ramo Hospital de Jesús, Archivo General de la Nación, Mexico City.

9. On encomendero society in early central Mexico, see Himmerich y Valencia, *Encomenderos*; Ruiz Medrano, *Reshaping New Spain*; and Altman, "Spanish Society."

he concluded his campaign in 1531 than Guzmán began to establish Spanish towns, making Compostela, near the Pacific coast, his capital, although already by the mid-1530s many Spaniards preferred Guadalajara, which later became the capital of Nueva Galicia and official seat of the audiencia (although in fact the audiencia judges never took up residence in Compostela). Other towns were founded as well, San Miguel in the north and La Purificación in the south. Guzmán assigned encomiendas to Spaniards who had participated in the entrada, reserving the most substantial and wealthiest communities for himself and a few of his captains and assigning some to his associates who had not participated in the entrada but arrived in the area after its conclusion. These latter assignments especially outraged men who had suffered through the arduous campaign and received in reward small, remote, or otherwise unviable grants or nothing at all. Guzmán also alienated many of the would-be conquistadors-turned-settlers by delegating authority to men who abused their positions, mistreating Spaniards and Indians alike. A number of people simply left the region to return to Mexico City or to try their luck elsewhere.

The result of Guzmán's shabby treatment of many of his fellow Spaniards in the 1530s and the lack of any widely available profitable resources was a fragmented, restive, and numerically very small group of settlers frustrated by their poverty and the limitations on their ability to exploit the local Indians. Unlike the Indians of central Mexico, the peoples of the west for the most part probably were unaccustomed to providing tribute or labor duty to their lords on a regular basis. In contrast to central Mexico, where the well-established custom of delivering tribute and providing labor enabled Spanish imposition of the encomienda, in western Mexico the local inhabitants deeply resented and strongly resisted such demands. Probably only a very small number of Spaniards in Nueva Galicia benefited much from their encomiendas, Guzmán of course being one of them.[10]

---

10. As the reader will see in the last chapter of the volume, which focuses on the community of Xalisco, encomienda assignments of some of the larger communities could yield substantial amounts of labor and tribute. This was the exception, however, and clearly Spanish success in exploiting Xalisco's labor and productive resources hinged in part on the presence of the encomendero's retainers and, from time to time, on that of the encomendero himself and a long history of punishment

Desperate to find a way to make a living, some Spaniards lobbied for authorization to wage slave-taking campaigns in areas where the local people ostensibly resisted Spanish rule. From the time of Columbus's earliest voyages, the Spanish Crown had flip-flopped on the issue of Indian enslavement.[11] Ever cautious about staying on the right side of the law, when he became governor Guzmán initially refused to allow slave taking. In 1534 the Crown reversed its policy once again, however, allowing Guzmán to authorize slave taking in the region. In a series of campaigns in the mid-1530s, in which he and other prominent Spaniards participated directly, more than 4,600 men, women, and children were captured, officially branded as slaves, and sold, some as far away as Mexico City, although perhaps a majority ended up working in local gold mines that Spaniards were beginning to exploit. Spaniards found other means of obtaining slaves as well, either extorting them from local rulers or purchasing them from indigenous traders. The early focus on gold mining suggests one of the main reasons why Spaniards continued not only to be committed to settling the west but vied for control there: they were convinced that mineral riches would be found.

Far from pacifying the region, not surprisingly the slaving campaigns of the mid-1530s exacerbated hostility toward and resentment of the Spaniards. The indigenous peoples of the west did not belong to any large political entity comparable to the Aztec or Tarascan states. Instead, their communities for the most part were autonomous and independent of one another, in some cases maintaining good relations, in others maintaining long-term conflicts and rivalries. This political fragmentation offered them both advantages and

and intimidation. Barring a strong Spanish presence, some, perhaps most, communities refused to provide tribute or labor and even turned on their own leaders if they tried to make them comply with Spanish demands.

11. Queen Isabel rejected the notion of enslaving Indians when Columbus sent indigenous captives to Castile, hoping to make people a profitable export. Isabel objected on the grounds that the Indians were her vassals and therefore entitled to royal protection. Encounters with indigenous groups that resisted Spanish rule and Christianity, however, offered to Spaniards the pretext of enslaving Indians based on the doctrine of "just war." Although indigenous enslavement would be banned once again by the New Laws of 1542, in fact exceptions still were made through the eighteenth century, as Indians considered to be in "rebellion" continued to suffer enslavement as punishment, although the clergy worked to limit the terms of enslavement that could be imposed.

disadvantages in confronting the Spaniards. During the 1530–31 expedition Guzmán and his associates found to their frustration that not only did the apparent defeat of one community not necessarily mean that others would submit but even when a pueblo did submit its people possibly considered the act to be a temporary expedient that would last only until the Spaniards moved along. Even after Spaniards were able to establish themselves on a somewhat stronger basis in the region, their ambitions were constantly thwarted by the Indians' refusal to participate in the encomienda system except when threatened and coerced, their habit of absenting themselves from their pueblos, their lack of readily available wealth in the form of precious metals, and their pronounced disinterest in—even hostility toward—Christianity. Although on an individual basis perhaps a small number of Spaniards were able to negotiate a modus vivendi with the Indians, for the most part Spanish-Indian relations were characterized by mutual distrust and incomprehension, resentment, and brutal violence.

The Guzmán era in Nueva Galicia came to an end in 1536, when he traveled to Mexico City to greet the new viceroy, don Antonio de Mendoza. Although initially received courteously, Guzmán found himself imprisoned and charged on a number of counts relating to his conduct as governor of Nueva Galicia.[12] He was sent to Spain, where he lived another twenty years, never returning to Mexico. The man who Charles V sent to replace him as governor, Lic. Diego Pérez de la Torre, who arrested and jailed Guzmán, served only about a year in Nueva Galicia before dying of injuries incurred in suppressing one of many recurrent local uprisings. The choice of his successor, Francisco Vázquez de Coronado, signaled a major shift in the official view of the role that Nueva Galicia might play in the further expansion of Spain's American empire.

Despite the relative brevity of Guzmán's sway over the west, his campaign of 1530–31 resulted in the tenuous, contested Spanish occupation of the huge area that became known as the kingdom of Nueva Galicia. Although Nuño de Guzmán's personal ambition to

---

12. The charges brought against Guzmán as part of the *residencia*, or judicial investigation into an official's conduct in office, were almost entirely limited to his term in office as governor. In colonial Spanish America, *residencias* routinely took place at the end of the term.

unite his two governorships, of Pánuco in the east and Nueva Galicia in the west, under his authority in a jurisdiction that would be quasi-independent of Mexico City came to naught, nonetheless his effort to make Nueva Galicia an entity separate from the rest of New Spain had a lasting impact. In 1548 Nueva Galicia would acquire its own audiencia, in recognition both of its geographic distance from central Mexico and of the importance of the silver mines that Spaniards began to exploit on a substantial scale beginning in the late 1540s in the area of Zacatecas.

Not long before the end of Guzmán's governorship, in the spring of 1536 the arrival of a strange party of Spaniards in the remote Spanish outpost of San Miguel in Culiacan unexpectedly initiated another important chapter in the history of Nueva Galicia. Subsequently to become famous for their experiences living among the Indians of the Gulf Coast and Texas, Álvar Núñez Cabeza de Vaca, together with two other Spaniards and an African slave, were the sole survivors of a 1528 expedition organized and led by Pánfilo de Narváez to Florida and the southeastern region of the present-day United States. After contacting Spaniards in San Miguel, Cabeza de Vaca and his party traveled south to meet with Nuño de Guzmán in Compostela and then on to Mexico City to report to the viceroy.[13] The accounts of their travels (and travails) encouraged some Spaniards—not least the viceroy himself—to believe that rich civilizations lay well to the north of the current limits of Spanish settlement. The next man who became governor of Nueva Galicia, Francisco Vázquez de Coronado, was Mendoza's young and inexperienced protégé, only recently arrived from Spain. He was charged with the organization of a major expedition into the north that would seek out the ostensibly wealthy peoples there. The expedition, of which Viceroy Mendoza was a major sponsor, departed in 1540.

Although the numbers of Spanish settlers who left Nueva Galicia to participate in this expedition were fairly small, probably no more than a dozen, they included some fairly prominent local figures. Quite possibly their departure, along with that of Indians recruited

13. An extensive body of scholarship exists on Cabeza de Vaca, along with a number of editions of his account. To date the most exhaustive is Adorno and Pautz, *Cabeza de Vaca*. For a perceptive treatment of the account, see Reséndez, *Land So Strange*.

locally for the expedition, appeared to offer an opportunity for the increasingly desperate indigenous people of the region to assert themselves and expel all the Spaniards from their midst. In this sense, if not more directly, the Vázquez de Coronado entrada into New Mexico might have contributed to the last of the three major stages by which Spaniards ultimately consolidated their control over Nueva Galicia, although not before they faced and eventually overcame the most organized and widespread challenge to their rule they would experience anywhere in the Americas in the sixteenth century.

In mid-1540, as incidents of indigenous violence against Spaniards were becoming increasingly frequent and brazen, local Spaniards made a startling discovery. People from several Cazcan pueblos north of Guadalajara had been fortifying and supplying a site known as Tepetistaque, reportedly making common cause with the Zacateca Indians. The Zacatecas lived to the north in proximity to the Cazcanes but had not been brought under Spanish rule. Their collaboration with the Cazcanes certainly suggests that they understood the threat that the Spaniards posed to their own way of life and independence. Miguel de Ibarra, a Spanish captain and the encomendero of Nochistlan, one of the Cazcan pueblos, was in Guadalajara when he received word that don Francisco Tenamaztle, the brother of Nochistlan's ruler and a Christian convert, had departed with a number of residents from the pueblo and some outlying settlements. Receiving confusing reports from local rulers and interpreters, Ibarra organized a small group of Spaniards and led them to Tepetistaque, along with fifteen hundred ostensibly friendly Indians from the Tecuexe pueblo of Tonala and three thousand Cazcanes, who proved to be less than trustworthy allies.[14] Although Ibarra captured some of the Cazcan leaders, the Spaniards were unable to defeat the Indians defending the *peñol*, as the fortified stronghold was known. Ibarra and his men retreated to Guadalajara, receiving news of other attacks and disturbances along the way.

For well over a year Spaniards in Nueva Galicia experienced a series of defeats and setbacks as Indians participating in the uprising took control over the countryside, fortifying one stronghold

---

14. When Miguel de Ibarra questioned the Cazcan captives, he discovered there was a plot among at least some of the Cazcanes to turn on the Spaniards and attack them from the rear.

after another. When governor Vázquez de Coronado departed on the entrada to the north he left Cristóbal de Oñate in charge as acting governor. Even during Guzmán's expedition Oñate acted as a powerful man in his own right, probably enjoying a larger personal following than Guzmán himself. After the conquest he received in encomienda the substantial community of Xalisco. His reputation, influence and experience were such that many assumed he would become governor after the untimely death of Pérez de la Torre, but, as seen, Viceroy Mendoza had other plans. Notwithstanding that choice, Mendoza trusted Oñate to deal with the fast-growing threat in the west, even though the numbers of Spanish settlers remained very small, and they barely could count on any of the local communities to provide reliable allies. Only gradually did Mendoza become aware that local resources were insufficient to defeat the uprising, which steadily gained in strength as one community after another joined what became a huge and ethnically diverse coalition united in the common desire to eliminate the Spaniards from their homeland.

Although it is not possible to reconstruct a comprehensive narrative of the war during the first year or so, certain episodes stood out. One of these was the defeat in April 1541 of Cristóbal de Oñate, accompanied by around fifty Spaniards and an unknown number of Indians, in the first battle for Mixton. The Spaniards who laid siege to Mixton for several weeks misjudged not only the strength of their adversary but also the latter's ability to communicate with allies outside the peñol. With Spanish forces reduced by an assault by Indians from another peñol that drew off a number of men, they lost a battle during which the rebels burned and robbed their camp and killed thirteen Spaniards, six Africans, and more than three hundred native allies.

This victory was instrumental in expanding indigenous support for the rebellion, which began to spread beyond the Cazcan communities to the Tecuexe pueblos and others. Oñate urgently requested aid from Mendoza in Mexico City. The viceroy instructed don Luis de Castilla and Pedro de Alvarado, who were in Colima on the Pacific coast waiting to embark on a voyage of discovery to the South Sea (in which the viceroy himself had a stake), to take their men and go to the aid of the Spanish settlers in Nueva Galicia. By mid-June 1541 these men had arrived in Guadalajara. Reinforcements also began to arrive from Michoacan. Late that month, ignoring those who counseled caution, Pedro de Alvarado, famous for his role in the conquest of Tenochtitlan, took a large force of Spaniards and allies from Michoacan to attack the peñol of Nochistlan.[15] Rather than attempting to negotiate or lay siege, he led a direct assault. The response was a massed attack from the rebels, which caused the Spaniards and their allies to panic and flee, a retreat made more dangerous by muddy terrain. When Alvarado dismounted to lead his horse, another man's horse fell on him. Suffering mortal injuries, he was taken back to Guadalajara, where he died several days later.

The death of Alvarado had an electrifying effect on Spaniards and Indians alike. For Spaniards this shocking and pointless loss underscored the seriousness of the revolt and suggested the possibility that, if not suppressed, it could spread throughout New Spain. In contrast, the message the Indians of the west received was quite encouraging: they could defeat the strongest of their foes. The rebellion began to spread rapidly, reaching communities that hitherto had been unaffected. It should be noted, however, that support for the uprising was far from uniform. Some communities did not participate, and even within those that joined rebel ranks there often were individuals and groups that attempted to remain neutral or even aided the Spaniards, underscoring the complexity of indigenous sociopolitical organization and of relations both among Indians and between them and local Spaniards.[16] Following the war several Spaniards testified that they had received warnings from Indians to safeguard their property and families in face of imminent rebellion. Although we can only speculate why some people alerted their encomenderos to the danger they faced, the warnings are a reminder of the difficult decisions that people were forced to make.

The first turning point of the war occurred in September 1541, when Spaniards managed to defend Guadalajara, which had been

15. Pedro de Alvarado played a leading, if controversial, role as Cortés's second-in-command in the conquest of Tenochtitlan and went on to try his luck in Guatemala and subsequently Peru. See Restall and Asselbergs, *Invading Guatemala*.

16. There are many indications that communities in the west could be ethnically or politically divided and have more than one ruler, which might have fostered rivalries or at least a lack of unity, disposing one group to support the rebellion and another to refrain from doing so. People or groups within communities also might have responded quite differently to external overtures to join the rebellion, some viewing them with distrust because of their source. In the case of Xalisco the intimidating presence of Spanish strongmen probably sufficed to keep them out of the war.

besieged by some fifteen thousand warriors. A company of Spanish horsemen targeted an elite group of fighters, killing around one thousand and dispersing the rest. The last phase of the war began the following month, with the arrival of Viceroy Mendoza leading an army of Spaniards and Indians from central Mexico, reinforced by recruits from Michoacan. Mendoza's forces overcame one stronghold after another, and as time went on the viceroy was able to negotiate the surrender of some peñoles. Nonetheless, this last phase of the war was hard fought, culminating in the defeat of the peñol of Mixton at the end of 1541. By then probably the largest of the peñoles because survivors of other defeated strongholds had taken refuge there, Mixton gave the war the name that is commonly used. While no doubt its fall was the key to Spanish victory, the mop-up phase of the war dragged on another couple of months.

During the campaign Mendoza sought to maintain a balance between the need to reward his indigenous allies by turning captives over to them and his desire to reconcile the majority of the rebels to Spanish rule. The result was that, although Mendoza's forces returned to central Mexico with several thousand slaves, many indigenous rebels were allowed to return home and received amnesty, probably in exchange for their agreement to receive baptism as Christians and, of course, to acquiesce to Spanish rule.

Even with this relative restraint in enslaving or otherwise punishing the defeated rebels, the war was a traumatic upheaval that marked another stage in the disruption and undermining of indigenous society in the west that began with the entradas of Francisco Cortés and Nuño de Guzmán. Thousands died, while many survivors of the war, including the influential leader don Francisco Tenamaztle, fled northward into the mountains. Others were forcibly relocated. In contrast, from the Spanish point of view the outcome of the war was a success. Although it failed to put an end to all violence in the region, the defeat of the insurrection helped to establish Spanish rule in the west on a much more solid basis. Not until the early nineteenth-century struggles over independence would Spanish dominion again be so strongly and widely contested in Mexico.

With the exception of the Francisco Cortés expedition, the events briefly narrated here left fairly extensive records. There are multiple Spanish accounts of Guzmán's campaign of conquest, including Guzmán's own reports, although none of them offer a complete

description of events.[17] For the final uprising and its suppression
there is a fairly long but secondhand, incomplete, and frequently
inaccurate report from Jerónimo López, the questionnaire and depositions that were part of the viceroy's *residencia* (inquiry into his
conduct in office) conducted in the mid-1540s, and a good deal of
testimony about the causes of the war and specific events from eyewitness observers and participants. Almost inevitably, eyewitness
reports and testimony at times are contradictory, and they provide
an episodic rather than a complete narrative of the course of the
war. The war did not inspire anyone to set down a comprehensive
account, perhaps because it was notably lacking in dividends in glory
or wealth for the participants, including the viceroy. Not only did
Spaniards suffer defeat after defeat during the first year of the war,
but final victory under Mendoza's leadership yielded little in the way
of booty or rewards.

In addition to the Spanish sources, others that reflect indigenous
perspectives are of particular interest. These perspectives pertain
to two quite different groups of indigenous peoples, the Spaniards'
Indian allies from central Mexico and the peoples of the west. A fascinating chronicle of Mendoza's campaign during the Mixton War set
down at the behest of the indigenous ruler of Tlalmanalco in central
Mexico, who accompanied the viceroy during his campaign in Nueva
Galicia, reflects the experiences of Indians from central Mexico.[18] For
people in western Mexico the *residencias* of Guzmán and Mendoza
include indigenous testimony, mediated and problematic but nonetheless valuable and worth considering. There also exists an account
written or commissioned by the rulers of the indigenous community
of Xalisco describing their encounters with Francisco Cortés and
Guzmán and experiences under Spanish rule in the 1530s and 1540s.[19]

<hr/>

17. There are eight full or partial accounts of the Guzmán campaign of 1530–31,
differing considerably in length, detail, bias, and emphasis and sometimes contradict-
ing one another. Guzmán's letter to the Crown midway through the entrada and his
later "Memoria" also are important sources. They have been published in two edited
volumes, García Icazbalceta, *Colección de documentos*, and Razo Zaragoza, *Crónicas de
la conquista*. There are redundancies between the two collections, and all the accounts
in Razo Zaragoza's edition have been published elsewhere as well. Guzmán's "Memoria" has been published in *Cuatro crónicas*. I have relied principally on these published
sources for my translations, checking them against the originals where possible.

18. Sandoval Acacictli, *Conquista y pacificación*.

19. See Calvo et al., *Xalisco*.

Another document is attributed to one of the key leaders of the uprising, Tenamaztle, who escaped into the mountains at the end of the war but eventually turned himself in and was exiled to Spain.[20] The existence of multiple types of documentation that allow us to focus attention on the indigenous understanding of events is unusual for this early period of Mexico's history. Most accounts of the conquest of central Mexico that reflect indigenous views and experiences are retrospective, set down a generation or more after events took place and often compiled in collaboration with or under the supervision of Spanish friars. In contrast, don Francisco de Sandoval Acacitli's narrative of his experiences fighting alongside the viceroy in western Mexico was recorded at his initiative as events took place. The indigenous perspectives presented here through these accounts are supplemented in some instances by texts produced by Spaniards. This is especially true for Nuño de Guzmán's expedition because the only extant records are those produced by Spanish participants. Where there are no indigenous accounts, or they provide only an incomplete record of events, I have used the Spanish accounts that shed the most direct light on indigenous experiences. In some cases material that is redundant or adds little to our knowledge and understanding of events and circumstances has been omitted from the translations of these accounts.[21]

The story of the Spanish occupation of western and northwestern Mexico and the stubborn indigenous resistance that it met provides an important counterpoint to the triumphalist narrative of Hernando Cortés's conquest of central Mexico, affording a different perspective on Mexico's early history.[22] Initially, Nueva Galicia seemed remote and poor in contrast to central Mexico, lacking central Mexico's dense populations and highly urbanized centers. Nonetheless, following

20. León-Portilla, *Flecha en el blanco*, includes a good transcription of Tenamaztle's petition and deposition (*información*). The original document is in no. 11, legajo 205, Audiencia de Mexico, Archivo General de Indias (hereafter AGI), Seville.

21. The account of don Francisco de Sandoval Acacitli, for example, literally progresses day by day, meaning that many passages simply note where he and his people slept and when they departed for their next destination.

22. A growing body of scholarship suggests that "conquest" in the Americas was a far more complex and less straightforward process than once thought, as were its consequences and outcomes. For New Spain, see the articles in Matthew and Oudijk, *Indian Conquistadors*; for elsewhere in the Americas see, for example, García Loaeza and Garrett, *Improbable Conquest*.

Nuño de Guzmán's expedition Nueva Galicia began to attract interest from several powerful men and became part of the complicated politics of early Mexico in which the first viceroy, don Antonio de Mendoza, emerged supreme over all other real and potential rivals. His victory in the Mixton War was an important factor in the consolidation of his power—and therefore that of the Spanish Crown—in Mexico. Despite the region's apparent poverty Spanish commitment to occupying western Mexico persisted and indeed grew over time because of the potential for mining precious metals. Spaniards in the west began working gold mines, using indigenous labor almost from the outset. At the very end of 1546 the first substantial silver deposits were found in Zacatecas, not far to the north of the area that was the cradle of the great indigenous rebellion. Men like Cristóbal de Oñate who lived in the region and played key roles in suppressing the uprising became important figures in opening the silver mines of the north.

The pacification of Nueva Galicia was of critical importance in the establishment and expansion of silver mining in Mexico, but indigenous labor was needed for any and all enterprises the Spaniards hoped to undertake. This was the conundrum of the west: although the vitality and independence of indigenous groups posed a considerable challenge to Spaniards, they certainly did not want to eliminate them. Spaniards needed the Indians to be compliant with their demands, an objective that proved very difficult to attain. During their first ten years in Nueva Galicia, Spaniards thought that coercion, and perhaps conversion to Christianity, would transform the fiercely independent western peoples into the submissive labor force they sought. The Mixton War was the direct result of the enormous gap between the reality of local indigenous society and Spanish expectations. The association of Christianity with Spanish demands for labor and tribute imbued the uprising with a strongly anti-Christian quality. The people who joined the rebellion of the early 1540s envisioned no middle ground; they hoped to eradicate all aspects of Spanish society, including Christianity and its representatives, from their midst. In the end, many of the once-autonomous communities survived, but barely. They continued to contend with the demands of their masters, which were not alleviated by the introduction of the New Laws of 1542, which were intended to reform the encomienda and ameliorate the conditions in which the Indians lived

FIGURE 2 Map of Nueva Galicia in 1550, prepared as part of the visit of inspection conducted by Lic. Hernando Martínez de la Marcha, one of the judges of Nueva Galicia's new audiencia. The Pacific coast is at the bottom. Ministerio de Educación, Cultura y Deporte del Gobierno de España, MP-México, Mapas y Planas, AGI, 560. Reproduced in Altman, *War for Mexico's West*, 195.

and labored.[23] The region increasingly became home to people—Spaniards, Indians, Africans—who came from central Mexico to settle in the west. Perhaps more definitively than any of Mexico's other regions, Nueva Galicia was radically transformed to conform to Spanish objectives over the course of barely twenty years.

23. The New Laws represented the second attempt by the Spanish Crown to regulate conditions of indigenous labor, the previous one, the Laws of Burgos, having been promulgated thirty years before. Not only did the New Laws limit the use of indigenous labor through the encomienda, they again banned the enslavement of Indians and mandated the freeing of most Indians who had been enslaved. The New Laws were most effective in places like central Mexico, where there existed a substantial official apparatus to enforce them. The timing of the promulgation of the New Laws, coming so soon after the conclusion of the Mixton War, meant that probably many of the people taken captive as slaves and brought to central Mexico after the war subsequently were freed.

1

Tenamaztle's Lament

This letter from don Francisco Tenamaztle was written in 1555, while he was living in exile in the important north-central Spanish city of Valladolid, where he very possibly was held in a Dominican monastery.[1] The letter probably was the result of a collaboration between Tenamaztle and a Spanish clergyman, very likely the renowned defender of the Indians, fray Bartolomé de Las Casas, who was living in Spain during that time.

Tenamaztle was from Nochistlan, a Cazcan province in western Mexico. The Cazcan language was similar to Nahuatl, the language of central Mexico, perhaps sufficiently so that the two languages were mutually intelligible. Tenamaztle held an important position in Nochistlan; he was the brother of the lord and had his own following.[2] He was baptized by the Spaniards, receiving the Christian name Francisco. He served the Franciscans in Nochistlan as a religious aide in their church and monastery. Indeed, he was recognized by the Spaniards as the leader of the community and given the staff of office, which may suggest that his brother failed to come to terms with the newcomers. By the time of the uprising in late 1540, however, their roles seem to have reversed. Tenamaztle had become so alienated from the Spaniards that he left Nochistlan with his people to take refuge in one of the strongholds some Cazcanes had established in league with the still-independent Zacatecas to the north.

---

1. See León-Portilla, *Flecha en el blanco*. León-Portilla concludes that Bartolomé de Las Casas participated in the writing of the letter. The original dates from July 1555.

2. Tenamaztle may have been considered a secondary ruler. It was not unusual for communities in western Mexico to have more than one ruler.

Taken captive following one of the battles of the war, Tenamaztle escaped during a daring rescue carried out by his supporters and retreated north to the mountains. After nearly ten years he turned himself over to Franciscans, apparently hoping for reconciliation and amnesty. The bishop of Nueva Galicia, however, sent him to Mexico City, and from there he was sent into exile in Spain. What impact his letter and deposition had, if any, is unknown. He died in Spain soon after it was written.[3]

The language in which the letter was written (Spanish) raises questions as to its authorship. Possibly Tenamaztle spoke Nahuatl as a second language and in addition might have learned Spanish, either from the Franciscans in Nueva Galicia or during his time in Mexico City and years of exile in Spain. Did he collaborate on the letter with someone in Spain who knew Nahuatl, or had he become sufficiently proficient in Spanish that he was able to dictate or write parts of it himself? Some of the language closely resembles that of Las Casas and other religious figures who protested against and condemned Spanish treatment of the indigenous peoples of the Americas. At the same time the syntax and vocabulary in at least parts of the letter are very awkward, seemingly not the language of an educated clergyman. It is clear that Tenamaztle participated in some fashion in writing the letter, describing with great bitterness what he and his relatives and compatriots experienced at the hands of the Spaniards. These details appear in the letter.

> Very powerful lords,
> Don Francisco Tenamaztle, chief or ruler of the province of Nochistlan and Xalisco,[4] I kiss the feet and hands of Your High-

3. A series of payments authorized by the Council of the Indies in 1556 (Indiferente General 425 L. 23, AGI) shows that Tenamaztle was treated for an illness and died by October of that year. A payment of six *ducados* was made to Inocencio Núñez, *criado* of "don Francisco Tenamaztle" (fol. 245 recto), and other funds were designated for items he needed. In September 1556 twelve *ducados* were paid for his medical treatment (fol. 249 recto). A Dr. Peñaranda received four *ducados* "for his work in visiting don Francisco Tenamaztle, deceased, during his illness, which was from twenty-five of September until the fifth of this present month of October [1556]" (fol. 253 verso).

4. Xalisco was an important community in central Nueva Galicia and is the focus of chapter 4. Spaniards began to use the name to refer to a larger region, which is the sense in which it is used here.

ness and appear before this Royal Council of the Indies. . . . I have been sent to these kingdoms of Castile by the viceroy of New Spain, don Luis de Velasco,[5] a prisoner and exile, alone, dispossessed of my rank and lordship and of my wife and children, in all poverty, thirst and hunger and extreme necessity, by sea and by land, suffering many injuries and insults and persecutions from many people and with other many serious toils and dangers to my life. And for this cause I have been displaced, by which I have been greatly harmed, against all reason and justice. . . .

Because it has not been enough that the Spaniards have done to me so very many and irreparable outrages [that are] unbelievable for men of this world, making unjust and extremely cruel wars on me, killing many of my vassals and people and my relatives and kin, and running me off, forcing me to go fleeing and in exile from my home and country and wife and children through the mountains for many years for fear of those that plot against and persecute my life. Later, in the time of peace, if indeed it could be called peace and not actually cruel war, [they] wickedly and shamefully hanged many great lords, my vassals as well as relatives and friends.

The beginning and means of these losses and injuries [we] received was Nuño de Guzmán, who first came to my country, I being their ruler, not recognizing any other ruler in this world as superior, as the public enemy of my lordship and republic, violent oppressor of me and my subjects against all laws of nature and of peoples, being in my country and they secure and peaceful, [acting] as if it were against enemies [who were] already declared and defying the Christian people, or of the kings of Castile, that the universal church or his kingdoms would have gravely offended with great arrogance. To which I would justifiably have resisted with arms, with whatever force, as a man infamous as a tyrant, destroyer, and oppressor of the Mexican peoples and those of Pánuco[6] and Michoacan for the

5. Don Luis de Velasco succeeded don Antonio de Mendoza as viceroy of New Spain in 1552.

6. Nuño de Guzmán became governor of Pánuco, the region to the northeast of central Mexico, in 1527. He undertook extensive slaving campaigns, sending many captives to the large islands of the Caribbean. See Chipman, *Nuño de Guzmán*.

cruelties that he had done in those provinces, killing and tortur-
ing kings and great lords and many others without number so
they would give him gold and silver, as was the terrible cruelty
he wreaked on the king, the cazonci of Michoacan[7] and others
here and in other parts. . . .

Because I, the said don Francisco, wanted only to go out in
peace, ordering my people to receive the Spaniards in a gracious
and friendly way, and they gave them in great abundance the
supplies they needed and giving them a very good welcome
from a natural and excessive charity in which nothing more
could be done for them, putting myself in great danger that I
did from the very great evil and harm that later came to me
and all that belonged to me they did. He [Guzmán] later went
on to the province of Culiacan[8] to look for the gold and riches
they sought. He devastated that province, which was one of the
most beautiful and populous in the world, killing whomever
they found without respect to sex or age or status, wrecking
the houses of the people, children and old people, young and
elderly, setting them on fire and watching them burn alive.

Having destroyed that province, very soon he returned to
Xalisco, and to repay the hospitality that I and my people and
all the other rulers provided, with the [same] payment and
gratitude that they showed those of Pánuco, he decided to settle
there because our province seemed to be more in the territory
of gold and silver. And he placed me, the said don Francisco, and
my people and many other rulers and lords with their people in
the customary harsh captivity and servitude that the Spaniards
call encomiendas, distributing to each Spaniard the pueblos
and their residents, as if we were beasts in the field, however it
seemed best to him and his captains. And I and my people and
the other caciques[9] and people suffering with patience the said
captivity. And also the friars of San Francisco who later came

---

7. See chapter 2. Guzmán held the cazonci hostage and tortured him and others
in hopes of wresting treasure from him. He had him tried for treason and executed.
Michoacan was home to the Tarascan or Purépecha state, which was independent of the
Aztec Empire. See Warren, *Conquest of Michoacán*.

8. Culiacan is in modern Sinaloa.

9. Spaniards used the term *cacique*, which they learned in the Caribbean, to refer
to a native chief or ruler.

there told us that they had come to teach us that we should know the one and true God, the just and pious king of Castile [and] and only for that reason.

At this time I was one of the first who, as a result of the teaching and persuasion of the said friars, converted and received the holy sacrament of baptism, along with many lords and commoners. With all the pueblos being quiet and secure in these days, he [Guzmán] sent by night people on foot and on horseback to assault us, and all those whom they took—because they took whom they wanted—they made into slaves and with a brand that said they belonged to the king they ordered them branded. And in this fashion they made so many [slaves] that they were innumerable, men and women, children of all ages, leaving husbands without wives and wives without husbands, children without parents and parents without children; and thus they sent them to sell to the mines and in other parts of New Spain, wherever they would pay best.[10]

Besides that, the said Nuño de Guzmán and his retainers, being more merciless than others, and all the other Spaniards afflicted each of the pueblos and Indians whom they held with excessive work both in the mines and outside of them [and with] pitiless oppression, treating them with such severity in all manner of servitude and inhumanity, as if they were made of iron or metal, no more taking into account their well-being and lives than if they were wild beasts in the countryside.

The injustices and cruelties that Juan de Oñate and Cristóbal de Oñate and Miguel de Ibarra,[11] whom he made captains, committed in that kingdom [of Nueva Galicia] could not be imagined nor conceived. They hanged nine leading lords, others of my kinsmen, nobles, and principal vassals because as a result of the ill-treatment, whippings, and beatings and other

10. Guzmán and his captains undertook extensive slaving campaigns in Nueva Galicia from 1535 to early 1537, officially reporting the capture and enslavement of more than 4,600 men, women, and children.

11. Juan and Cristóbal de Oñate were brothers. Juan left the region in 1536, reportedly for Peru, but Cristóbal remained. He was the encomendero of Xalisco and became acting governor of Nueva Galicia when the third governor, Francisco Vázquez de Coronado, departed for the expedition to New Mexico in 1540. Miguel de Ibarra was active throughout the Mixton War and played a role in the opening of silver mines in Zacatecas, where Cristóbal de Oñate became one of the leading mine owners.

different evil, merciless, and insufferable bad treatment that the Indian commoners received, being unable to suffer any more such iniquity and wickedness, [they] fled to the mountains just as a gentle ox naturally will flee from the slaughterhouse. And they would follow them as a hunting party [and should they in] defending themselves hurt or kill some Spaniards, with the rulers and lords secure in their houses serving the encomenderos, they would hang them for what certain people had done. And in this fashion for these reasons they hanged many rulers and nobles, increasing every day the injuries and irreparable harm, calamities, harsh captivity, deaths, and depopulations we suffered, then arriving by sea the *adelantado* Alvarado and five hundred men going to discover [the South Sea islands], who were lodged in that province. And those discoveries were made by many Spaniards in territory whose people were afflicted by outrages after outrages, evil after evil, robbery after robbery, and violation and rape of married women and daughters who were taken, and other uncountable [acts], that everyone in those lands knows is true, which is the sole custom and habit of the Spaniards wherever they go in these Indies.

And so, all the kingdom being afflicted, oppressed, weary, destroyed, and those who remained in such a beaten-down and calamitous state that they did not doubt their utter end and destruction, as so many innumerable thousands had been destroyed, if the said servitude, contrary to all natural justice to be free people commended to the Spaniards, as we are, continued, they resolved to flee to the mountains and fortify themselves in order to defend their own lives and those of their women and children, given that God and nature concede this natural defense even to the beasts and to things without feelings, and all the laws, divine and human, favor and defend [them] and hold them as legitimate.

And I, don Francisco, seeing how inhumanely and without justice all the nine rulers, being secure in their homes and lands, had been hanged, and many and innumerable vassals of mine had perished, not remaining of all the *vecinos*[12] of that king-

---

12. The term *vecino* has varied meanings. In the sixteenth century it usually meant a citizen or head of household, but here he seems to be using the term more generally to refer to residents. It also, as today, could mean neighbor.

dom one in one hundred, there being no justice nor means to obtain it, nor anyone to whom to complain or ask it, because all were and are our sworn enemies because they all robbed and afflicted and oppressed and tyrannized us, as to this day they do, I decided also to escape with the few people who remained to me, to save them and myself, as by natural law one is obligated, because if I did not flee I too, with the same injustice and cruelty, would be hanged. That flight and natural defense, very powerful lords, Spaniards, misusing their words in all the Indies,[13] call and have always called rebelling against the King. . . .

I was in flight and hidden for nine years, where if I did not wish it, no Spaniard would ever see or find me. But remembering that I was a Christian, and going through the mountains I could not continue to be a Christian or live or rest, believing also that in coming from where I was safe to my own land and lordship that I inherited from my parents and of which I had been despoiled and deprived, without just cause nor reason nor was I acknowledged, I came alone and of my free will to offer myself to the bishop of those provinces[14] so that he could deal with the Spaniards, [thinking] that I would be received with friendship and humanity and Christianity. . . .

The bishop told me that he thought we should go to see the viceroy don Antonio de Mendoza as the person who would be served by my return. I told him that I agreed with good will. And thus we came to Mexico City and found that he [Mendoza][15] already had left, and don Luis [de Velasco] had arrived as successor in his place.

I was there one year with the bishop. At that time he died, and wishing to return with his priests to my home, the viceroy detained me, and without any reason or new justification beyond those which I have already described, had me arrested and put in chains and taken to Veracruz to embark and bring

13. At this time the Spanish commonly referred to the Americas as *Las Indias*, from Columbus's mistaken conviction that he had found a route to Asia.

14. The first bishop of Nueva Galicia was Pedro Gómez de Maraver, who arrived in the province in 1547 and died several years later.

15. Don Antonio de Mendoza was the first and longest-serving viceroy of New Spain, from 1535 to 1551. Although Mendoza was in poor health and exhausted, the king sent him to serve as viceroy to Peru, where he died in 1552.

me prisoner here [Castile] with outrages and abuses, hunger and thirst and debasement of myself, which I already have begun to address. . . .

I ask and entreat Your Highness that, having before your eyes only God and the truth and justice, and [given that] I am a Christian and that the hard persecutions and intolerable damages, plunders, captivities, pursuits, and exile that I and mine have suffered and those of us still alive still suffer, and the misery and misfortune in which I am presently unjustly placed, you order remedied and have justice done in the following things.

First, that because if I made a criminal complaint about those who contrary to natural justice law have done against me so many deaths and arrests, offenses, insults, and harm, however many, Your Highness, they would not order [them] killed; and if I did or I made a civil accusation that they should pay and satisfy said harm and damage, neither they nor all their lineages would suffice, even if they had great incomes and rank to satisfy me and the other rulers and lords and all that kingdom and its vecinos who are the aggrieved and injured ones.

In order to spare my complaint and also the danger to my life and person that I suffer being in a country so different and [more] extreme in cold and heat than mine where I was born and brought up . . . trusting in the rectitude and equality that this Royal Council of the Indies also uses in the prosecution of justice . . . Your Highness will hold that it is good to order that the vecinos and residents of the pueblos of Nochistlan and Xuchipila and their subject communities be put at liberty, ordering that I be reinstated in their lordship as something that is properly mine and that my parents left me and from which I have been dispossessed; and that Your Highness should incorporate me and all of them in the royal Crown of Castile, in whose devotion and service I wish always to live [and] those who succeed me and under the royal banner each and every time to serve as a vassal, for which I will do homage according to the customs and laws of Castile.

And in fulfillment of that I will work to attract to the service of the royal Crown the Acatlecas [Zacatecas] and Coachichiles [Huachichiles], which are other nations that are wild and have not come to the service of God nor obedience to Your Majesty, that for the great harm and evil that they have received from the Spaniards, for those that have heard of [what] their neighbors and the provinces where the Spaniards have arrived have suffered, and many other pueblos are hidden, fierce, and in mortal hatred and enmity of them because of their horror of what they have perpetrated wherever they arrived. All these I offer to bring, without lances or swords, Your Majesty giving me a bishop and some friars with whom I would go from here and there proclaim and preach as the priests [do] in other places and make good the will of Your Majesty. And of the grant that would be promised to do and will do for them the most important is—and I put this first as a condition for my complying of what I would offer those nations—that Your Majesty give me a letter and royal provision and guarantee for them with all the force of privilege and justice that one can place [on it] that all the pueblos and peoples that I bring to peace and who by my effort come, from that time will be incorporated into the royal Crown of Castile and that at no time and for no cause, reason, or necessity, while they are true to their oath and devotion to the kings of Castile, will they be removed or commended to Spaniards or any other individual nor given in fief nor by any other means that can be conceived. And that the rulers and natural lords will remain and be maintained and confirmed in their rank and lordships, and their heirs will succeed them in conformity with the just laws and customs that they have, always recognizing as supreme and sovereign the lords and kings the universal kings of Castile.

Don Francisco Tenamaztle

2

Spaniards Conquer the West

The first organized expedition, or entrada, into western Mexico was led by Francisco Cortés, a kinsman of the much better-known Hernando Cortés, the conqueror of central Mexico. Francisco Cortés organized this expedition under the authority and sponsorship of Hernando Cortés while living in the coastal enclave of Colima, whence they departed in 1524. Although Cortés's party did not venture north of the Río Grande de Santiago, Hernando Cortés later would argue that he had a legitimate claim to settle the region that his kinsman had traversed. During the year following the expedition, Cortés sent two men to do a survey of the communities Francisco Cortés had contacted, but the Spanish presence in the west, north of Colima, remained minimal. As a result, it would prove impossible for Hernando Cortés to demonstrate that this entrada resulted in any real Spanish settlement.

Nuño de Guzmán undertook the next Spanish foray into the west. He was both president of the first audiencia of New Spain in Mexico City and governor of the northeastern province of Pánuco. Most of what we know about this expedition into the region that the Spanish would call Nueva Galicia comes from a series of accounts by participants and Guzmán's letters and reports. Most of these firsthand accounts date to 1530–31 and so are nearly contemporaneous to the events reported. The expedition left Mexico City at the very end of December 1529. Along with several hundred Spaniards, Guzmán conscripted around eight thousand indigenous warriors in central Mexico for the expedition and an equal number when he arrived in Michoacan.

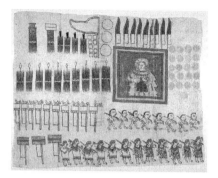

FIGURE 3 Plate from the Codex Huejotzinco, showing the banner that Guzmán had the people of Huejotzinco make for his entrada. Harkness Collection, Manuscript Division, Library of Congress, Washington, D.C.

When Guzmán left Mexico City at the end of 1529, he took with him the cazonci, or native ruler, of Michoacan, whom he had been holding hostage. Spaniards had taken over the Tarascan (Purepecha) kingdom of Michoacan in the early 1520s, but for a few years they ruled indirectly through the cazonci. When Guzmán's party reached Michoacan, they delayed there for over a month as Guzmán attempted to extort treasure from the cazonci, whom he later tried and executed. He also demanded supplies and men in addition to those he had brought from central Mexico (see his letter of July 8, 1530). Not only did Guzmán's expedition include thousands of indigenous warriors as well as other auxiliaries and porters who had been forcibly recruited, but some of the Spaniards who accompanied him were unwilling participants as well. His campaign was unpopular with them because they saw it as an unnecessary provocation of hostilities in a region that, although not yet occupied by Spaniards, was at peace. Although none of the surviving accounts of the expedition are indigenous in origin, whether for their own reasons or because they genuinely sympathized with the Indians, some of the authors of the accounts were critical of Guzmán and portrayed the experiences of the Indians in sympathetic terms. Cristóbal Flores, probably one Guzmán's captains, made his negative opinion of Guzmán clear in the account he offered to the judges of the audiencia in Mexico City.[1]

1. The account attributed to Cristóbal Flores has been published in Razo Zaragoza, *Crónicas de la conquista*, 181–213. In the nineteenth-century compilation of García Icazbalceta, *Colección de documentos*, it appears as the fourth anonymous chronicle. I have omitted some sections of the account, most notably those dealing at some length with Guzmán's treatment of the cazonci of Michoacan, as it lies somewhat outside the focus of this volume.

Very reverend and magnificent sirs, you saw fit to command that in order to serve His Majesty I should make an account of the conquest and war that Nuño de Guzmán undertook, as someone who for two years accompanied him, because you were certain that being zealous in his royal service I would do so truthfully and in the manner that it occurred, both in the things that happened to us up until the time that I left [to return] to this city where I have my house and citizenship [*vecindad*] and in the damage that was inflicted in passing through the peaceful communities that were entrusted [to him] and of the treatment that the said Nuño de Guzmán dealt to the vassals of His Majesty whom he took with him, both Spaniards and the natives of this land, and of the death of the cazonci don Francisco, lord of the province of Michoacan, and of the treatment of other lords his vassals whom he took with him and the order by which he waged war in those provinces and how it occurred that he first engaged in battle with the natives of that place and if he established peace with them and other particulars that touch on the manner of the war and good and welfare of the land and of the conversion of the natives. All this you charged and ordered me as a man who was with the said Nuño de Guzmán for the entire duration of the war, so that His Majesty would be informed of the truth as from a good vassal. And although you might consult other persons who have come [back] and are better chroniclers than I, . . . I will recount as briefly as I can what I remember and will do so with all truth, without missing a point of what has happened, as you will see in the following.

You will know that Nuño de Guzmán left this city in pursuit of his expedition on December 20, [15]30.[2] For the number of Spaniards whom he took with him I refer to the muster that passed before Alonso Lucas, his secretary; for the number of friendly natives of the land that he also took with him I refer to García del Pilar, who provided a list of them all.[3]

2. This year should be 1529.
3. García del Pilar also provided an account. He was a well-known interpreter of Nahuatl in early Mexico who had worked with Cortés. He quickly became estranged from Guzmán and was another one of his critics. For a translation of his account, see

Making our daily marches toward Michoacan, on the third day we slept in a pueblo called ____,[4] which the maestre de Roa held in encomienda, where [the people] from fear of our arrival and of the many allies who accompanied us abandoned their houses. And from anger that they did not bring us food and because they left their houses, Nuño de Guzmán ordered that they be sought along with the friendly warriors that we brought, with their arms and devices, as if the Indians of that pueblo were in rebellion and at war. And [as] there was no lacking those who said how badly it was done, he sent Peralmindez Cherinos and Juan de Burgos to bring back the allies, and they returned. And because of his anger at a cousin of the maestre de Roa, who was in that pueblo, believing that it was his fault that the Indians fled, he ordered that a chain be placed around his neck, and he kept him that way for two days, until [we reached] another pueblo called Istlabaca, which Juan de Tovar held in encomienda, which also received some damage as a result of our passage.

From there we did not cease our daily marches until [we reached] the city of Uchila, which is the capital of the province of Michoacan. Before we arrived in the city, the Indian governor, don Pedro, came out with many people, natives of the land dressed in their battle finery, to do service and pleasure to Nuño de Guzmán, and with this festivity he entered to take lodgings in his quarters in the city.

Then he called on the lord who was named don Francisco and in his language the cazonci, who had been prisoner in this city [Mexico City] for a long period before he left, for what reason I could not say. He [Guzmán] brought him to this city, as if he were free but very secure and well guarded, and ordered him to have eight or ten thousand of his vassals gathered to take with him for the war he was beginning to make; and he responded that he would do as commanded. And three or four days after he ordered that, he had him put in chains and placed in a small room next to his own room on the pretext that he

---

Fuentes, *Conquistadors*, 197–208. The indigenous allies recruited from territories under Spanish control were known as *indios amigos*.

4. This space is apparently blank in the original account.

guzmā.   michv aca.

FIGURE 4 Guzmán in Michoacan. A modern rendering of an illustration commissioned by the second viceroy of New Spain, don Luis de Velasco, in the 1550s. Chavero, *Lienzo de Tlaxcala*.

had not brought sufficient supplies and food for the people he brought with him. In addition, he ordered his retainer Godoy, who was chief magistrate in the province, and his interpreter García del Pilar to ask why had he not prepared the gold and silver that he had been ordered [to provide] in that city. The said cazonci replied that he had collected it already and most of it was collected. . . .

[After about two weeks, during which Guzmán failed to extract the treasure that he was convinced the cazonci was hiding, he had the ruler tortured by fire. Ten days after that the Indians that Guzmán had demanded were brought.]

Each ruler of a town came with the portion of his subjects that had been assigned by the *repartimiento* [allotment of labor], all of whom were divided up by the Spaniards who went to war so that they would carry their goods; and for security that these Indians would not flee and leave their belongings, the lords and nobles marched with chains around their necks, and many of them died prisoners. Taking don Francisco as prisoner, we left that city. . . .

And so we continued our march to the river that he named Nuestra Señora, two leagues beyond Purandiro, the last town in Michoacan; this river is the boundary of the land at war. There we took out the banners with all the footmen and horsemen, sounding the trumpets and ordering it proclaimed that as president of New Spain and governor of the province of Pánuco he took possession of those lands, as can be seen in the proclamation, and on a promontory had the allies build a church surrounded by a wall crowned with battlements and doors like a fort. On the pretext of waiting for this to be completed, he waited for Godoy and certain lords of Michoacan who were there to come with a certain portion of the estate of the cazonci and women, who arrived. This I saw because at a turn of the river I received two ladies, one of them very highly placed, a relative of the cazonci whom Juan Pascual, Nuño de Guzmán's interpreter, handed over to me out of pity to see her badly treated. I sent her in a hammock to her land with her maids and certain Indians who were her vassals. . . .

[Subsequently, Guzmán accused the cazonci of having ordered the killing of some Spaniards living in Michoacan and continued to torture him and two of his interpreters. Flores took pity on the latter, giving them wine to drink after they were released. They were tortured again, however, as were several nobles, including don Pedro Panza, second in authority to the cazonci. Guzmán had the cazonci tried and sentenced him to death, following which he was tied to the tail of a horse and dragged, then burned at the stake despite his protests to the end that he had been loyal to the Spaniards.]

After having been at that river more than twenty days experiencing want, we left there for a pueblo called Cuinao, taking with us don Pedro Panza, the governor of the province; and two interpreters, all of whom had to be carried in hammocks because of the condition they were in from the torture. We went that way downriver for a few days through an unpopulated area until arriving at Cuinao. And there we entered at war because the natives had fled in terror and did not wait for the Requirement.[5] [Guzmán] decided to make an expedition to some other nearby pueblos, and then when we returned this pueblo of Cuinao agreed to peace. . . .

Having left Cuinao, we went looking for another pueblo called Cuiseo, which is at the edge of a river that goes from a lake to the northern sea between Xalisco and Centequipaque.[6] Before we arrived at this river, near its headland there was a squadron of warlike Indians against whom Nuño de Guzmán sent Juan de Burgos and myself. When they saw us coming toward them with the rest of the people behind us, they left the bank of the river, which was very deep, placing their arms on the ground, signaling that they wanted peace. Nuño de Guzmán arrived and ordered the field marshal Villarroel and others to make rafts to cross over to them. He ordered the cacique Tapia, a lord of Mexico, to bring wood and fasteners for them, which his commoners made. And because the said cacique, who was ill, did not enter the water there and help them to make [the rafts], the field marshal treated him such, handling him roughly, that he never was well again until he died. And so by making those rafts and firing the artillery they made peace and sent an interpreter to swim across the river, and that night we slept there.

The next day we went downriver looking for a ford until we found one and crossed to Cuiseo, which was at the river's cape. That day some of the natives of the pueblo died because they abandoned the pueblo and went to fortify themselves on an island in the river, and some Spaniards were wounded. After five or six days that we were moving through the area of this pueblo there approached a fat Indian peacefully who by his manner appeared to be a lord. And because he did not bring *tamemes*[7] for the party, or what Nuño de Guzmán had asked,

---

5. The Requirement, or Requerimiento, was essentially a legal document explaining to the Indians that they were "required" to recognize the sovereignty of Charles V and accept the Catholic faith. Should they do so they would be allowed to live peacefully, although under Spanish rule; if they failed to do so the Spaniards could wage war on them and take them captive.

6. The Spaniards named this river the Río Grande de Santiago. It marked the northern limit of Francisco Cortés's entrada of 1524.

7. Flores uses the Nahuatl term, *tamemes*, for bearers or porters.

he ordered that he be set on by dogs; and thus very bitten and mistreated we left him at the door of his lodging, burning the pueblo. This burning continued wherever we went. Given that Nuño de Guzmán ordered that we try hard to keep the pueblos from being burned, notwithstanding this, the native allies we brought were such that although they were burned alive, they would not desist from burning wherever they went, with no way to prevent it.

From there we went in search of Tonala, and also there were many allies in chains so that they would not flee and leave their packs, by consent of Nuño de Guzmán. And after two days' march we arrived in the province of Tonala, and once we were in sight some Indians came out peacefully with hens in their hands, saying that the lady of that province was peaceful and in her house and that the majority of the pueblo wanted to serve the Spaniards, as did the other provinces; but certain relatives of the *cacica*,[8] along with many of their other principal subjects, were on a hill for the purpose of fighting the Christians. And with this we entered the pueblo and found the *cacica* in her house with many of her vassals and belongings and birds. . . .

[The Spaniards marched on the Indians who were on the hill and attacked, forcing many of the defenders to flee. They remained there almost three weeks, pacifying the area, and then went on to Nochistlan, where they spent another twenty or thirty days and failed to make peace with any of the communities. The Spaniards' allies continued to burn pueblos, leaving the area desolate. Soon after that Guzmán split the expedition into two parties, one led by Peralmindez Cherinos and the other by Guzmán himself, heading toward Xalisco.]

Arriving in a large pueblo called Aguacatlan, which is in a very populous valley, the Indians came out to [greet] us peacefully. We lodged in their houses, and they provided us very well with what we needed. And here Villarroel hanged one of the allies for a certain crime, or later in another pueblo, I cannot remember. In Aguacatlan Nuño de Guzmán demanded gold and silver from the natives, and they gave him some and some women and also gave him around a thousand *tamemes* to carry

---

8. A *cacica* is a female ruler.

our belongings. And not happy with this, he ordered that the lords be seized, and in addition to receiving this harm in their houses, some died as prisoners. And I saw ____⁹ in the chain in which the lord of another pueblo was tied.

From here in five or six days we arrived at a pueblo called Xalisco, where we found the inspector [Peralmindez Cherinos], who had come by another route. When we passed through it a certain part of the natives of the pueblo of Xalisco had retreated to the mountain and it was at peace.

From here we passed to the pueblo of Tepique, which was peaceful, about a league and a half ahead of Xalisco. There Nuño de Guzmán chose the royal officials, the treasurer, accountant, factor, and overseer. We were in that pueblo a month, and the lords of Xalisco came there in peace and with food, to whom it was indicated that they should give a certain quantity of tribute. Many of us believed, but I am not sure if it is so, that because they were unable to comply they rose up, and this the interpreter, Rodrigo Ximón, Nuño de Guzmán's *criado* [servant or retainer], will know because he dealt a good deal with them and told them what they had to do. And because of this provocation Nuño de Guzmán ordered that war be made on them and proclaimed it [to be] of fire and blood and ordered them given as slaves, although later they did not brand the majority of those they took. The day that Nuño de Guzmán left with his company, the pueblo was completely burned, and from there we went as far as the South Sea [Pacific], which he took possession of [by] entering in it, and passing through the area we returned to the pueblo of Tepique.

From there he sent the captain Cristóbal de Berrios with certain footmen and horsemen to look for a ford in the great river that goes down from Cuinao and passes between the lands of Temoaque and of Tepique. [Having] found [it], he passed to the other bank, where he encountered many warriors, and as a prudent person he retreated with his people and returned to make an account of everything to Nuño de Guzmán. There he ordered that two Indians be hanged because they wanted to return [home]. And then he made good his departure for that

9. This space is blank in the document.

river and province that was on the other bank; we spent four or five days going and crossing to the other bank, and [with] all the horsemen ready, he ordered the trumpets to be sounded and proclaimed that he ordered all the scribes and notaries, under [threat of] a certain fine, that from that river onward they should call [it] Mayor España in all the writings they did.[10] And then he put his hand to his sword and cut certain branches of trees, taking possession, and he asked a notary to attest to it. Then advancing a little we encountered warriors who were hidden and ready to fight with us, where fifty or sixty horses and some of the Spaniards were wounded. After they were defeated, continuing the pursuit, we returned to lodge in the pueblo of Temoaque. I cannot remember if a Requirement was made before waging battle with the warriors because the first to engage in it, because of [having] sent us forward to explore the countryside, were Villaroel, the field marshal; Gonzalo López; and the *alcalde*, Samaniego; and myself as witnesses of that.

From here in two days we departed for a pueblo that is called Omitlan, where we were a month and a half, waiting until certain peaceful Indians came, and so Nuño de Guzmán could send his account to Castile and await news from ahead, where we would go.

Leaving here to go to seek the province of Aztatlan, after seven or eight days we arrived in it with much effort because of the many marshes along the route, in which a good horse [belonging to] Nuño de Guzmán drowned. Having arrived within sight of the settlement, which is on some plains on the shore of a river, many warriors came out to receive us, and because we could not pass them that day because of the obstruction of another river that was ahead that we could not pass, they carried off their property and fled to safer places, and the next day we went to stay in the pueblo, where we spent the winter and were there for a long time until the rains had passed. Here the former *oidores* sent him [Guzmán] a messenger with a certain dispatch, letting him know about the

---

10. Charles V was not pleased with Guzmán's choice of Mayor España, which seemed to suggest that the new lands would be greater than Spain itself, and rejected the name.

arrival of the *marqués* [del Valle de Oaxaca, Hernando Cortés], although he already had known this in the previous pueblo, called Omitlan. From here he sent to that city [Mexico City] the inspector Peralmindez Cherinos with up to ten horsemen.

Spending the winter on the shore of that river, during certain days in September such a great storm of water and wind came up that it took most of the houses, and so great was the amount of rain and the river swelled in such manner that there was not a house that was not half submerged in the water, from which we all thought to perish for [its] having hit us at midnight and for the land having proved [sickly] for the allies we brought with us. Many of them were lying ill in their huts; they drowned and were carried away by the water. After the storm passed, as all the rest were sick and exhausted, all the rest of them fell ill, including the *naborías*[11] who served the Spaniards. The mortality was such that of the multitude of allies that we had I do not believe that five hundred remained healthy, and some of them fearing death and for other reasons, the storm having carried away our food and many of the hogs, they fled to return to their homes even though they knew that they would be killed on the way. And to intimidate them, so more would not leave, Nuño de Guzmán had some of those who wanted to return [home] hanged. Regarding this you should take testimony from García del Pilar, who knows more or less how many, because in talking about how bad this seemed he told me that he remembered who had been ordered to be hanged because they wanted to return [home].

The lord of this city of Mexico, named Tapia, and the lords of Tatilulco [Tlatelolco] and Tlaxcala and Huejotzinco and many other lords and principal men from this province of Culhua, seeing how poor their health was and how there did not remain to them a vassal who had not died, and other needs they experienced, they went to beg and ask for mercy from Nuño de Guzmán that for the love of God, since all their people had died he should take their jewels and battle finery and allow them to go back to Xalisco, which was healthier country, to pass

---

11. *Naboría,* another term that Spaniards picked up in the Caribbean, means servant or dependent.

the winter. After asking them who had allowed them to ask permission, he would not give it. And I know that none of those lords who went to ask escaped; they all died. And seeing such great mortality, he sent those who were strongest and all who could walk to march [north] toward the province of Chiametla with two captains on horseback. And because it was unpopulated [land], with many marshes, the mortality was such that we could hardly move along the road, and from pure desperation they hanged themselves ten by ten.

Before leaving Aztatlan he [Guzmán] hanged a Spaniard who had been brought by force from the province of Michoacan because he left, and they brought another who left to be hanged, and at the pleading of others he was brought back from the gallows. Here for some days he kept prisoner and tortured certain hidalgos because he thought they wanted to return. And by this you can consider how he treated Spaniards and Indian allies. Witnesses to this were the maestre de Roa and Martín López and Francisco de Carranza and García del Pilar and other vecinos of this city that went in his company. . . .

[Having lost so many people and most of their supplies, Guzmán decided to send his field marshal Gonzalo López, along with fifteen or twenty horsemen and again as many footmen back to Michoacan "to bring Indians and cattle and Spaniards by force or whatever means possible." Guzmán sent one of his close associates together with interpreter García del Pilar ahead to Chiametla, where the people received them peacefully, offered supplies, and sent some men to carry the Spaniards' belongings. Being unaccustomed to such labor, however, they abandoned the packs and fled; that, along with some other offense, turned the people of Chiametla against the Spaniards. Guzmán stayed in Aztatlan awaiting the return of Gonzalo López and after a month and a half sent García del Pilar to look for him. He found him in Aguacatlan, which had previously been subdued, branding slaves. Flores maintained (and other accounts confirm this) that in addition to the Indians López brought from Michoacan, he took captive men, women, and children from several communities, including at least one thousand from Xalisco and another five hundred to one thousand from Zacualpa, where not only had the lords been arrested when they came out to greet the Spaniards peacefully, but their Indian allies had killed or sacrificed another two thousand people with the Spaniards' consent.]

I also learned for certain that being in Xalisco with all the prisoners from these pueblos together to be branded, the natives of Xalisco, understanding the deception, began to flee, so only two hundred remained. And angry about this, the field marshal Gonzalo López seized the principal lord of Xalisco and burned him alive. Witnesses are the above mentioned. And it is said that when they had branded all the Indians that they had taken from these peaceful pueblos, all tied together with ropes around their necks, they made their way to where Nuño de Guzmán was.[12] The people who went with him said that all the little children and the women had died or were killed on the road, which was the greatest pity in all the world. . . . Subsequently, the Indians who had been brought in peace from the towns of the *marqués* [Hernando Cortés] and of Alonso de Ávalos, which at the time belonged to Manuel de Guzmán, and from other pueblos, were divided up among the Spaniards. I would say that just as one would rent out beasts, so these poor Indian allies were handed out to the Spaniards like household goods.[13] I point out Francisco Barron and Villas and García del Pilar as witnesses to that. Also after the slaves who had been taken here in peaceful territory, with compensation for each person one peso of gold, thus we departed that province, leaving it at war and mistreated, first sending Francisco Verdugo to settle Xalisco.

Traveling another four or five days, we arrived at a small pueblo that was subject to a main town that was toward the sea, named Quezala. Here two Spaniards who had left Chiametla ill had requested permission to return with Francisco Verdugo to peaceful country, because they were so sick, [and] he would not give it to them. Here we were four or five days making some

12. This episode took place during a time that the Spanish Crown had banned the enslavement of Indians, but Guzmán contended that the people of these pueblos had "rebelled" by damaging Spanish herds and property that had been left behind there. Thus he argued that waging war on them and taking slaves was justified.

13. Here Flores is referring not to the people who had been captured and branded but rather to the reinforcements that Gonzalo López was sent to conscript and bring back from Michoacan or Colima.

small forays and to see if any province would come to him in peace. Always many Spaniards from his company continued to try to return because he was so harsh with them.

Leaving here, traveling we arrived at a settlement that was called [the place] of the beans, where we stayed fifteen days and could not find a route because up until there the natives of Chiametla had opened it for us.

Leaving here looking for a route and traveling five days, we arrived at the province of Piaztla. This pueblo is near the South Sea, where we were for five or six days, and it never made peace. Leaving it destroyed, we departed. And from there many of the allies wanted to return. Learning this, Nuño de Guzmán ordered one burned alive, and I heard it said that he had ordered hanged I don't know how many. Notwithstanding this, a squadron of Indian allies [tried to] return . . . [but] were killed by the enemy, with the exception of one who escaped fleeing and came back to us. From here we left for another large settlement that is on the banks of a river, three leagues ahead, which we named the pueblo of salt, because there was a great deal of it in it.

From here traveling ten [days], passing through some warlike pueblos and never pacifying them, we arrived in the pueblo of Cihuatlan, which is the head town of certain pueblos around it, of which we had received notice, and it was said to belong to Amazons. In this pueblo and others that we passed through around it only women could be found and very few or almost no men, and so it was thought likely that they were the women we had heard about. And the reason that no men were found among them is that the men were leading parties in order to make war with us. So it is, because when we returned from the mountains and unpopulated area that we could not penetrate, we found them in their houses with their wives and children, no different than in other pueblos. It never was possible to find an interpreter who could understand them. This pueblo, head of the small province of Cihuatlan, is on the shore of a very good river close to the sea. In this pueblo he [Guzmán] hanged a Spaniard named Aguilar because he wanted to return as a result of mistreatment that he did to him, that serving as a cavalry captain he made him dismount and serve in a company on foot, and because of this affront and shame that he received he wanted to leave, and he hanged him. And so we left here, the land remaining at war. . . .

[Eventually they reached the area of modern Sinaloa, where they found lush and densely populated river valleys. Guzmán founded a town he called San Miguel de Culiacan, which was the northernmost outpost established by the expedition. A number of Spaniards and their indigenous auxiliaries stayed behind there, the latter not willingly, as Cristóbal Flores describes. Ten years later Culiacan would play an important role as the base for the expedition into New Mexico led by Francisco Vázquez de Coronado. From there Guzmán sent a party led by Gonzalo López to explore the mountains and plains beyond, which turned out to be unpopulated as far as the Spaniards could learn.]

The said Gonzalo López returned to Nuño de Guzmán very exhausted and thin, both he and his companions, and he told him that they had traveled one hundred leagues, crossing the plains one way and another and had not found a single settlement or heard of one, and had it not been for some maize that they left buried, they all would have perished from hunger. And that there they left forty or fifty bushels of maize and five or six Spanish horsemen to guard them. And [he said] that if they continued to try to go there he and all who went with him would have perished, that it all was unpopulated, that he should consider what he did.

On top of those mountains one hundred or two hundred of the Indian allies mutinied, of whom none escaped except four or five who arrived here and conveyed the news of how we were going through the mountains dying of hunger and half destroyed. Here also a Christian with a well-trained horse mutinied, and nothing more was heard of him.

With the return of Gonzalo López to make his account to Nuño de Guzmán, there was much discussion about it. Given that we did not have the supplies to continue on, nor was there anything ahead, he agreed that we would return to the province of Culiacan . . . and found a town there and, once done, go to Xalisco to found another and another in El Teul. As we all saw that that was his intention and there was nothing else to be

done, we answered that what he said was good and we agreed
with his view, thanking him for what he gave us. The next
day we turned back toward the pueblo of the Guamuchiles,
from which we had left, where we arrived very weary and in
much need. In that pueblo Nuño de Guzmán ordered two allies
hanged because they wanted to return to their country and
also in that same pueblo some blacks fled from their masters.
Before we returned from the mountains to that pueblo Nuño
de Guzmán sent six or seven footmen and some horsemen to
call and collect the Spaniards Gonzalo López had left on the
plains guarding the maize; and after a few days they followed
us to a pueblo, where they founded a town with great effort
because of hunger, as neither had they found anything to sustain them nor could we kill the hunger until we arrived there,
leaving some forty horses that had fallen. And on this return
[journey] many of the Indian allies perished as well as natives
of that land who we brought tied up, women and men for our
service by Nuño de Guzmán's consent, who died from having
nothing to eat nor was anything found but grass and weeds.

Having returned to this province and arrived at a pueblo
named ____,[14] where a town was founded, and having two or
three months that we were there founding it, as I have said,
he named it the town of San Miguel and had *alcaldes* and
regidores and an *alcalde mayor* and captain named Diego
de Proaño elected. And after consulting with the *cabildo*[15] many
times, it became known among us that Nuño de Guzmán had
given permission to take slaves and that each vecino could have
a certain number with which to collect gold and also with the
natives of the land, given that it was a new land and the vecinos
were much in debt. This was generally known among us, as I
say, and he then left a record for his lieutenant, so that after he
left it would be publicized and shown to all the vecinos, which
was in this manner: so and so would be served by such pueblo
so that they would build his house and feed him, as soon as the

14. This space is blank in the document.
15. The *cabildo* was the municipal council. *Regidores* were town councilmen and
alcaldes or *alcaldes ordinarios* were local magistrates of the first instance, normally
elected by the *regidores*. The *alcalde mayor* acted as district governor.

land was visited and a *repartimiento* (distribution) were made. In this way he did the *repartimiento,* some two by two and others alone, according to the quality of person. And many caciques, lords of peaceful pueblos, having arrived and their names written, he [Guzmán] left there after having been three months occupied in doing this, and he went to create the towns of Xalisco and Guadalajara.

Leaving in that town with his license and consent many of the Indians from this country [central Mexico] whom he had taken with him to help make war, in payment for their good service and work at the end of two years in which they traveled the roads and mountains loaded down, every day making huts and looking for food for us, he [Guzmán] left them in that town among the vecinos, free men made slaves, chained by the neck or in stocks so that they would not follow us, shouting and weeping when they saw us leave, because of the great wrong that was done to them in repayment for their work. And with no charitableness for that, he left for Xalisco. Witnesses [to that were] Pedro de Carranza, Luis Napolitano, Francisco Guillén, Martín López, the maestre de Roa, Alonso de Villanueva, García del Pilar, vecinos of this city [Mexico City].

This province is, from this perspective, the most populous I have seen on the Ocean Sea and the best furnished with supplies of maize and beans and chilies and fish, [and] very abundant with cotton. The natives are by far the most comely, especially the women, that in all the country on the Ocean Sea more beautiful and comely have not been seen. Their clothing is a shirt that reaches the feet, worn as a surplice with a loincloth underneath. The men cover themselves with mantas[16] but do not cover their privates; savage people without order, most of the men very tattooed. In all this province to the Espíritu Santo River there is grass. They are great archers. In no reserve or park of any lord in Spain have I seen such hunting of hares and deer and jackals as in this province. There are many markets where they deal in cotton cloth and fish and fruit and things to eat; there are few hens. They have good large houses with large porches covered with branches in front, where the

16. A manta is a cotton cloth or blanket.

women weave their cloth, and the walls of the houses are [made] of very large mats because of the great heat, because this is very hot country, more so than the island of Española. Their custom is to carry their loads and provisions on a thick bow; just as there are some [bows] for shooting arrows, there are others to carry loads on their shoulders, a net tied to one side of the bow and the other on the other side, and in this net they put what they wish to carry and in that way they walk. There is no lack of mosquitoes.

Of all the Indians that were brought from Tascaltecle [Tlax-cala] I don't recall that any escaped except two nobles who went chained, guarding the pigs of Nuño de Guzmán.

Flores ends his account with a brief description of the expedition's return south and the encounter with don Luis de Castilla, who had been sent by the audiencia to found a town, either near Xalisco or Tonala (accounts vary). Guzmán had his captain Cristóbal de Oñate arrest Castilla and send him back to Mexico City. During Guzmán's absence a new audiencia had replaced the first, meaning Guzmán no longer was president, although he still was governor of Pánuco, and the king appointed him governor of Nueva Galicia as well. Although he remained governor of the newly claimed territory for another five years, the questions raised about his actions during the expedition, especially the execution of Spaniards and the shockingly high mortality among the Indian allies, including the indigenous lords, resulted in the new audiencia's soliciting accounts and depositions like the one made by Cristóbal Flores and contributed to the Crown's loss of confidence in him.

By way of contrast to Flores's account, the following is taken from the letter that Nuño de Guzmán wrote to the king, from Omitlan, July 8, 1530, halfway into the expedition, before the disastrous flood at Aztatlan. It is highly self-serving, emphasizing his personal accomplishments, and not surprisingly casts his actions in a positive light.[17] The report is long and includes lengthy descriptions of his efforts to spread Christianity and his indignation at the uncivilized nature of the Indians. It is translated here in part.

17. The letter appears in Razo Zaragoza, *Crónicas de la conquista*, 21–59. The original is in Patronato 184 R. 10, AGI.

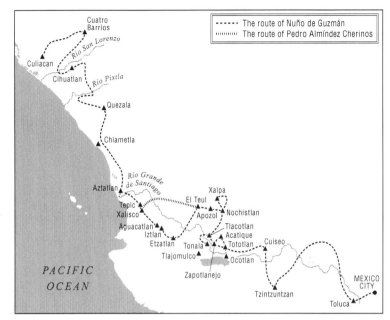

MAP 3 Route of Nuño de Guzmán's expedition

Because it is a new country and one of faithless idolaters, where so much service to God may be done, it seemed [well] to me to compose an account of all that would be done on this journey and everything that occurred in conquering this land, as well as declaring the quality of the land and its peoples and customs. From Michoacan I wrote to Your Majesty, after having written from Mexico [City], how I came with one hundred and fifty horsemeñ and an equal number of infantry, well armed, and with twelve pieces of light artillery and with seven or eight thousand Indian allies and provided with all [necessary] supplies, to discover the land and conquer the province of the Teules-Chichimecas,[18] which borders New Spain, and those

18. The term *teul* is adopted from Nahuatl *teotl*, which refers to a strong, powerful being (not necessarily a god, although it often is translated as such). Spaniards adopted the term "Chichimeca" from the Nahuas and, after the conquest of Nueva Galicia, used it to refer to the more mobile groups that lived in the region, especially in the sierras. Although in Spanish the term *Chichimeca* came to refer to groups they considered to be savage or barbarian, in Nahuatl it originally seems to have more positive connotations associated with warriors.

[lands] that lie beyond. I arrived at the crossing of the river of
Our Lady of the Purification of Saint Mary, which name was
chosen for having crossed on that day [Candlemas, February 2];
and because it was the first enemy territory, I decided to have
three large crosses that I brought already carved and made
which, after having said Mass, with a procession and trumpets
I with the captains and others carried on our shoulders, with
one placed above the river and another in front of a church
of Our Lady, which was called Santa María de la Purificación,
which they began to build, and another on the road that would
be taken. To all of them, with the greatest possible devotion,
worship was made. Thus was begun the raising of the standard
of the cross of Our Lord Jesus Christ in the land of the infidels,
which never before then had been placed, nor had Christians
been in it. Then some pueblos came peacefully to serve, and
this way we finished the church and surrounded it with a wall
so that within [it] fifteen or twenty horsemen could lodge. In it
was said the Mass and sermon, and having finished the Mass,
some ordinances for the good order that should be maintained
in the army were read. On February 7 [1530] possession of the
new discovery was taken in the name of Your Majesty and on
the fourteenth of the month the usual Requirement was made.
In this way I sent two cavalry captains to reconnoiter the land,
in order to see where to make the entrada.

Also, because of complaints and accusations that I had been
given regarding the cazonci, the lord of Michoacan, and by
virtue of a report that had been made of [his] having brought
the land to rebellion and agreeing to kill us if they could,
I proceeded against him. And having found that [report of]
the uprising was true and what they intended to do, and other
great and serious disservices and enormous crimes that he had
done, sacrificing Indians and Christians, as he had done before
becoming Christian, I sentenced him to burn, as will be seen
from the trial that was conducted. . . .

The captains having arrived and knowing the route that
should be taken and made muster of my people, I left, leaving
in that fort, which it is for the Indians, a Spanish resident of
Michoacan, and I went six days through an unpopulated area,
half of them downriver, leaving at each stopping place a cross

erected, and on the sixth day I arrived within two leagues of a
province called Cuinao, with good-sized settlements and abundant food, which we had begun to need very much. The day
before I went there, which was Saturday, February 20, I sent
Peralmindez Cherinos, Your Majesty's inspector and my lieutenant captain general, who is the captain of thirty horsemen,
to reconnoiter the land and the enemies and see what people
there were, because I was told they were hostile, and to require
them to come in peace, and the comendador Barrios with him
for the same purpose. Arriving, he found some warriors to
whom he made the Requirement, and the[ir] response was to
go up into the mountains. Of those who were slow, the horsemen captured some, not without protecting themselves. This
done, the inspector entered the place and found no one, and
upon their returning that night I sent messengers to say they
should not fear, that they should come to their houses to serve
and give obedience, that I wanted nothing else from them. They
sent to me by way of reply that they would wait for me with
their bows and arrows the next day. Thus I departed Sunday
morning, having formed three squadrons, both of Spaniards
and of Indians, and when I arrived at a large arroyo in front of
the place where I thought they were waiting for me, I found no
one, at least not there, because when they saw the order and the
many people that I brought, they did not dare wait.

In that place the people and horses recovered with the abundance of maize and other supplies from the land that existed,
and that day after eating I sent the inspector one way and
Captain Cristóbal de Oñate with his horsemen the other, and
I with the officers followed them. The inspector found no one
other than women and children. Cristóbal de Oñate found up
to one hundred men with their bows and arrows, who turned
on them and wounded two horses and three men, although it
was nothing dangerous. And some of them died [and] they captured others and many women and children, altogether some
five hundred people who were collected so the Indian allies
would not sacrifice them as they do. I was there preparing the
people and horses until Thursday, always sending messages to
the cacique that he should come in peace, because they told me
he had retreated to another nearby province called Cuinacaro,

which has a different language and lord. Seeing that he was not coming, I went to look for him because I was told he had many people with him, leaving in the camp Captain Francisco Verdugo, an honorable man and very senior conqueror. Passing that same day through [open] land and mountain, the runners saw many warriors on the slope, and our [Indian] allies killed some. I put the people in order and followed the route that they said they took, and I never ran into them, the woods being very dense.

I entered the other province that I mentioned, where there are many villages and an abundance of maize and fruit trees native to the land and where we found dead a great many people from the previous province who had retreated there [and been] sacrificed, and many ovens with their meat that they are accustomed to eat, which did not disgust our allies, although some of them said they were lambs, as later I will tell.[19] Some people from that province, both men and women, were found there whose language no one understood, and many more from the previous province. They wear beards of straw. . . .

[Guzmán goes on to recount a number of encounters, skirmishes, and military successes in addition to his determined efforts to spread the Christian faith.]

All these aforementioned provinces have a great deal of maize and beans, gourds, hens, parrots, and palms; it is country where they grow and make much cotton and with many people. It is believed, according to the disposition and location of these provinces, that it is a land of gold and silver, because it was found among some of the natives. Because iron tools and other necessary things were lacking, I resolved to return to the camp, where I arrived on Tuesday, the day of carnival before Ash Wednesday, and there I worked at trying to get the cacique to come. As he came with all his people and nobles, I received him well and made a speech, making him understand what was God and the pope and what they needed to do to save themselves, and how the king of Castile was God's minister on earth and the lord of all these parts, whose vassals they were, and that to me in his royal name they should give obedience and service,

19. Note that Guzmán is suggesting he saw evidence of cannibalism, something that Cristóbal Flores never mentions.

and if they would desist from sacrificing and worshipping idols and devils, as until then they had done, because only God should be adored, feared, and served and in the land, after him, to serve and obey the king of Castile. He told me that until then he knew nothing of that nor had he heard it, but that now that I had declared it he was glad to know it and he would do thus, and that thenceforth he would hold the king of Castile as a god and would worship him. . . .

[Guzmán responded by explaining that the king is a mortal, although the lord of all of them, and further elaborated on the benefits of worshipping the Christian God. His letter went on to describe more violent clashes and their efforts to cross the river.]

Among the people who in this island [of the river] defended themselves, a man dressed in women's clothes fought, so well and courageously that he was the last that they captured, of whom everyone was amazed to see such valor and strength in a woman, because it was thought that it was so because of the garment she wore. And after being captured it was seen that he was a man, and wanting to know the reason that he wore women's clothes, he confessed that since he was a boy he was accustomed to do so and made his living with men from that, at which I ordered that he be burned and it was done. After that I returned to the camp and sought to have the principal lords come and they came, although very fearful [because] of what had happened. I pacified them and gave cotton blankets to them and all the people who had been captured, some of whom went unwillingly, especially the women. After having ordered them to return to live in their houses, I gave them to understand, as to all of them is given, that I came to take possession of those lands on behalf of the king of Castile.

[Guzmán continued at some length about the need to Christianize the people of that place. His party advanced to Tonala.]

I set up camp on the slope of a hill near the river, whence messengers on behalf of the lady of that province, because there is no lord, came to me to say that she already knew of my arrival and that she awaited me with good will to receive me in peace and give me from what she had, although her neighbors, those who were on the other side of the river, which

were three provinces, Cuiula, Coyutla and Cuinacaro, were
crazy and did not want peace; and that since yesterday they had
come out to make war on her because she wanted to receive me
peacefully. . . .

[Guzmán divided his forces into three squadrons, and there
followed a fierce battle.]

Those who have found themselves with these people in New
Spain and other parts, they deem that they have not seen more
daring or courageous Indians than these. The arms they bore
were bows and arrows and *macanas* and two-handed swords
of wood and some slings and shields, very feathered and dyed,
that they intend to come [looking] very ugly, although they are
not themselves beautiful, appearing like devils so as to put fear
into the Christians. . . .

Then all the lords and people of that land came to serve and
give obedience and bring much food. . . . This is very good land,
very populated and with many provisions, and I believe that
having made an agreement with one pueblo in these parts, the
rest [of them] will serve. All that land is temperate, they have
many temples that were demolished, and they are great sacri-
ficers. They deal in silver and some gold and cloth, although at
first they denied it, and at present I do not show any desire for
it nor that I came for it; although they said that they will give
it, I have ordered it said that I do not need gold but rather that
they should be good and serve and not sacrifice. . . .

[Guzmán later would go to some lengths to try to extort
gold from the people of Nueva Galicia, as he had from the
cazonci of Michoacan. Searching for gold mines was one of his
highest priorities even during the expedition itself. Another
priority was spreading the faith, whether from genuine conviction or in hopes of ingratiating himself with the king—perhaps
both. He halted the expedition to observe Holy Week.]

It being Holy Week and in land [near Xalpa] where maize
was abundant, I decided to observe it there and to hold Mass in
a church that was built in one day of reeds covered with straw,
very pretty, with a cross in front and a good-sized altar in the
middle. And another was placed on the ridge on top of a *cue*
[temple] that was there, from which [it] could be seen from all
over the land. The office was celebrated as best we could, and

for war [time] and in such places quite well, and the building of the newest fashion that has been seen, because everything was of precious feathers. There were five hermitages for the stations, with some large crosses that remained in them, and on Holy Thursday a procession of more than thirty devotees took place. . . .

Guzmán's letter, written before the flood at Aztatlan, ended on a positive note. We know from the account of Cristóbal Flores that the expedition's troubles were only beginning. At its conclusion, Guzmán became governor and established several towns. Nueva Galicia nominally came under Spanish rule, but Spaniards quickly discovered that the autonomous communities of the west and northwest could not be governed as easily as the large political units of central Mexico that had been brought under Spanish control. Disorder and conflict were constant during the 1530s. In addition, Spaniards who had participated in the expedition were frustrated with the outcome; there was little wealth to commandeer, and many communities resisted Spanish attempts to impose encomiendas. In the north especially they resorted to plundering Indian communities, resulting in greater disorder, as seen in this description of what occurred in the town of San Miguel de Culiacan.[20]

The Spaniards neglected to plant and began to buy maize from the Indians and to trade with them for it, as well as the other foods they needed, because what the Indians contributed was not enough to sustain the Spaniards and their households; and when the Christians had exhausted the maize as well as the things with which to buy it, the captain [Proaño], not knowing [how] to provide a system by which the Christians could support themselves without destroying the land, allowed the Christians to take it forcibly from the Indians' houses, and after taking the maize they took blankets and beads, which are those turquoises, and other things they had in the way of possessions,

20. "First Anonymous Account," García Icazbalceta, *Colección de documentos*, 294. Guzmán left one of his captains, Diego de Proaño, in San Miguel as the district governor. Not only did Proaño exacerbate hostilities with the local Indians, but he also sowed so much conflict and bad feeling among the Spanish settlers that many of them fled.

in such way that the Indians, seeing they would not keep the peace with them, decided to flee and hide what they had in the forests and mountains and burn their own pueblos, which they did; and rather than try to make good this damage, the Christians began to pursue them and to rob the land, as they already had fled, and started to destroy it as it now is, and the Indians died of hunger, because they stopped planting for two or three years. . . . Given that now they have discovered rich mines, the Christians can support themselves in that town; and because of this a captain who does not know how to manage such a good land, as populous and extremely abundant as it was, does not deserve what others merit who know how to do it [properly].

3

Insurrection and War

After enduring a decade of abuse, exploitation, and slaving campaigns, a number of Indian groups in Nueva Galicia came together in a concerted effort to expel the Spaniards from their lands. The first to rebel were the Cazcanes, whose pueblos were in the area north of Guadalajara. They allied with Zacateca Indians, who lived in the mountains to the north and were not under Spanish rule. Later other groups joined as well, resulting in the creation of a large, interethnic coalition to eliminate the Spaniards from the west. The conflict, today known as the Mixton War, often has been depicted as a spontaneous uprising. There is, however, evidence of considerable planning, organization, and effective communication before the rebellion, as people had been meeting and fortifying and supplying high mountainous strongholds, known as *peñoles*, for some time without the knowledge of Spanish settlers and officials.

Part 1: The Origins of the War

The following report by the viceroy, don Antonio de Mendoza, reflects the Spaniards' understanding of the causes of the war.[1] His account must have been based on the reports and testimony of others, since he was not in Nueva Galicia for most of the first year of the war.

---

1. Pieza 3, Justicia 259, AGI.

The Indians of Tlaltenango, which is more than sixty leagues from Compostela, being quiet and calm and having established a monastery of Franciscans in Juchipila, some Indians from the mountains of Tepeque and Zacatecas came to some pueblos near Tlaltenango . . . with the devil's speech that they call *tlatol*.[2] They arrived at Tlaltenango, where they got together the lords and nobles and commoners, to whom they spoke, saying we are messengers of the devil who is called *tecocoli*,[3] and we come to let you know that he is coming and brings with him all your ancestors restored to life and with many riches and jewels of gold and turquoises, feathers and mirrors, bows and arrows that never break, much cloth with which to dress yourselves, and many beads and other things for the women and to let you know that those who believe and follow him and abandon the doctrine of the friars will never die nor have want. The old men and women will become young and will be able to conceive [children] no matter how old they are. And the fields will be prepared without anyone touching them and without rain, and the firewood from the woods will come to your house without anyone carrying it. Whoever goes to the woods after the devil has come will be eaten by jackals and mountain lions. When someone leaves the house to enjoy himself, whenever he returns he will find the food cooked without anyone having done so, and when the gourds are finished they will once again fill up with very excellent food. And the fish that you toil to catch in the streams, every time you lose one [another] very large one will jump out of the water and not what you normally catch and in all other kinds of food . . . you will enjoy what the devil has to give, which is much better. And the same [will be true] of the shields and arms that you had, because the devil will give you others that are much better, and he would bring beautiful small silver rings for your noses and the paint that they are accustomed to using on the face. The ones that the devil uses will never fade. He will give them many jewels to put in

2. Tlaltenango and Juchipila both were Cazcan pueblos. *Tlatol* means "statement" in Nahuatl, the main language of central Mexico. It might have referred to chanted as well as spoken words.

3. *Tecocoli* probably is from the Nahuatl *tecolotl* (owl).

the noses and ears and bracelets and cuffs for the arm. And they should know that the very flesh that falls off other immortal flesh he will replace and that the children that the women who have worshipped the devil bear, when they are born can beget [others]. The devil will give to each his woman, and the Indians will be told that they can have [all] the women they want and not just one as the friars say, that they should be happy with one until the hour of their death. And they should know for certain that the Indian man or woman who believes in God and not in the devil will no more see the light and will be eaten by wild beasts. . . . And then the devil will go to Guadalajara and Xalisco and Michoacan and Mexico and Guatemala and wherever there are Christians they will turn on them and . . . kill them, and with this done the devil will return to his home, and they will remain very content with all their ancestors engaged in what is mentioned above without working fields or other tasks.

One of the most detailed descriptions of the planning and activities taking place in some indigenous communities was offered by Hernando Martel after the war.[4]

This witness, being in the pueblo of Xalpa, the cacique and lord of that pueblo, who is called Aboaquinte in his language and in Spanish don Diego, and other *nahuatatos* of that pueblo many times told this witness that the Zacatecas came from far away and said to them, what are you doing and why is it that everyone does not rise up, and do they want to live in servitude? . . . and that they recognize neither king nor Spaniard, and no doubt they must be the willing servants of the Spaniards since they carry their loads and cultivate their fields, [and] that they had come from far away and there was something divine in the gourd. . . . Why did they not rise up and rebel, what about their past? [and] that he was angry that they did not give him hearts and blood as they were accustomed to do. . . . And for this they assembled them and called to them to rebel and speak

4. Response to question 132, pieza 3, Justicia 261, AGI. In 1547 Martel testified that he was twenty-five years old, originally from Seville, and had lived in New Spain for about twelve years.

to the lords and nobles of the pueblos that were at peace. And the said cacique said to this witness that he laughed at what they said, giving him to understand that he would not do such things nor even think of it. And that at times this cacique was missing from the pueblo of Xalpa for three or four days, and when they asked for him they said he was sick and that he was in his fields, and that some *nahuatatos*, wishing him ill, came to a Spaniard who was in the pueblo as the tribute collector and to this witness [saying] that he told them that he was gone and that he went many times to some dances [*mitotes*] that took place in the valley of Tlaltenango outside the pueblo so that the master of the pueblo would not know about them or the tribute collector there, in which dances they said that a very large part of the caciques and lords of all the pueblos and districts that were at peace gathered [and] in which dances was said to appear that which came in the gourd and that from that which came they received a great reprimand. And that each dance would last three or four days, and at other times they had the dances in Juchipila and at times in Tlaltenango itself, and there a very large part of the Zacatecas assembled and other times in Moquetabasco, a pueblo subject to Xalpa. And that in those dances everything that took place would conclude with their rebelling and killing all the Spaniards and taking their women as their mistresses, and it would turn out well when they were brave. And that they say that it would be enough not only for Nueva Galicia but for all of Mexico and that they were having these dances and pacts for more than two years, and they said that their ancestors would revive.

Tomás Gil testified that he had witnessed *mitotes* near the pueblo that he held in encomienda.[5]

This witness heard many Indians in Tanabita, which he holds in encomienda, and those of the pueblo of Juan Pascual and the

---

5. Responses to questions 132 and 154, microfilm roll 6, Justicia 262, AGI. In 1547 Gil testified that he was a vecino of Compostela, thirty-five years old, a native of the town of Zorita in the district of Trujillo in Extremadura, and had been in New Spain for seventeen or eighteen years.

pueblo of Omitlan, because he traded and moved around among them and saw the disturbance and dance and the speech of the devil, all of which they did and performed in front of him. . . .

At the time of the uprising this witness was in his pueblo, which is near the mountains of the Zacatecas. As he was alone the said Indians paid no attention to him and in his presence performed the said dance and speech of the devil, and he saw the messengers with the arrows with beads and amulets and [they were] of colors and a very large gourd to the sound of which they did the dance. And this witness broke it, for which they wanted to kill him. And they told him to go because they wanted to rebel.

Juan Hernández de Ijar, a longtime vecino of La Purificación in the south, testified as follows.[6]

This witness being captain of the district of La Purificación the Indian Antón, lord of Iztlan, and the Indian Pedro, native of Oloco, and Alonso, brother of the cacique of Iztlan, and many other leading Indians of the whole land told him that the Cazcanes and Zacatecas who were rebelling and especially those [people] of Atengoichan spoke to them, persuading them to rise up and rebel against the Christians, that the devil commanded it and with three arrows they would kill all the Christians of this New Spain and those who came by the sea and those from Castile. And that now it was no longer necessary to plant maize other than one day in the morning to plant, and at midday it would be green and at night could be harvested. And this witness heard them saying with his own ears abominations and following another, new way of being diabolical, [which is] throwing water on their private parts, saying that was baptism.

While a message of millenarian revivalism that was specifically anti-Christian as well as anti-Spanish seems to have been spreading, it more likely was a catalyst and perhaps a rallying cry for people who fiercely resented Spanish rule than the actual cause of the war. Many of the Indians of the west had not accepted their new Spanish masters,

6. Pieza 2, Justicia 261, AGI.

or had done so under coercion. Testimony taken from indigenous leaders who received amnesty after the war appears to confirm that emissaries from groups committed to expelling the Spaniards from the region visited other communities to recruit them to the cause. It should be recalled, however, that testimony compiled after the war not only was mediated by Spanish interpreters and notaries but also reflected the conditions under which indigenous leaders received amnesty at the hands of the Spaniards. Don Pedro, the lord of the pueblo of Tetitlan, swore by the cross and stated his age was twenty. Pedro Ruiz de Haro, a notary, acted as interpreter for his testimony.[7]

> At the time of the uprising, certain Cazcan Indians whose names he does not remember came to this witness and with them don Juan, the lord of the pueblo of Izatlan, which was held in encomienda by Alonso López. [They tried to persuade him] to rebel with them against the Christians and [said] that they were going to kill them all, and they said it to all the rest of the pueblos of this province and that of the Cazcanes. . . . It is true that this witness and the people of his pueblo rebelled with them. . . .
>
> And that neither this witness nor anyone from his pueblo ever received bad treatment from their master or any other Christian, nor did they ever learn that other pueblos of this province received mistreatment from their lords or from another Christian, rather many times among themselves they discussed how content and serene they were, and they learned the Christian doctrine. And this witness sent to inform his master that he should take from the pueblo of Tetitlan the cattle and property that he had there so that the Indians would not take it. And this witness found out that don Juan, the lord of Aguacatlan, had warned Alonso Delgado and Francisco Pérez to leave that pueblo so they would not be killed and in order to save their property.

7. Responses to questions 132, 137, 154, 155, pieza 2, Justicia 262, AGI. The Indian whom don Pedro mentions as having been sacrificed must have been the messenger that don Cristóbal of Xalisco sent to Tetitlan (see chapter 4), an incident which Alonso, identified as a *nahuatato* and noble of Xalisco, also mentioned in his testimony. Another don Pedro, described as lord and governor of a "certain part of the pueblo of Tetitlan," also testified that an Indian from Xalisco and "another Indian from Juchipila who had been raised among them" were sacrificed in his pueblo (pieza 3, Justicia 262, AGI).

Don Juan, lord of Iztlan, and the said Cazcan Indians came to this witness and led him to understand . . . that if he did not rebel, the devil's fire would come and encompass everyone, and they also made him and all the Indians of the pueblo of Tetitlan understand that they should wash their heads and put on . . . a black ink with which they dye themselves, and this would remove the baptismal water. And this witness, seeing the words and inducements of the devil's speech, was afraid, and they rose up with the rest of the rebels and made war on the Christians. And also the said Indians brought some arrows wrapped in hide as a sacrifice and gift and made them understand the *tlatol* of the devil. And this witness saw that a noble named Quechul, native of the pueblo of Tetitlan, with all the people whom he was in charge of renounced the faith of the Christians and returned to that of the devil, and thus he heard very publicly among those participating in the war that all the rebel caciques had done so. . . .

This witness while in his pueblo and in his presence [saw] an Indian sacrificed as in times past, and he found out and saw that in contempt of the sacrament they raised tortillas of maize . . . and cursed the images of Our Lady and other saints and threw them on the ground and sat on them. . . . And this witness with people from his and other pueblos saw them burn churches and a monastery.

Alonso, a noble of Juchipil in the valley of Aguacatlan, testified:

I saw the Indians who came with the *tlatol* . . . one of whom was named Horney, a native of Tequila, for which reason and because of the said *tlatoles* all the Indians of this province rebelled and this witness with them, believing that what it says in the question had to be true regarding the coming of the ancestors and death of Christians and for this reason the Indians of this province did very little planting.[8]

While it is clear that in much of their testimony the indigenous witnesses were responding to prompts from their Spanish

8. Response to question 132, pieza 2, Justicia 262, AGI.

questioners, or were pressured to state that they had never been mistreated, or because they had received amnesty were trying to provide
the answers they thought the Spaniards wanted to hear, nonetheless
one should not assume that all of their statements were compro-
mised. Given that all these witnesses testified through interpreters,
however, the extent to which the testimony recorded reflected their
actual words is uncertain. A man named Hernando Coyotlytomio,
a native of Tequila, for example, testified through two interpreters,
Spaniard Bartolomé González de Mendoza and Alonso, "nahuatato de
la lengua de México."[9] He is recorded as saying that "the messengers
from the Zacatecas and Tlaltenango made this witness and the people
of his pueblo understand . . . that their grandparents would revive,
and they would kill the Christians, and they would not have to work
because the maize and other seeds would grow . . . and many other
spells. . . . And this witness has seen that it all was and is a mockery
and lie what they told them about the devil, although when they told
it to them they believed it, and for that they suffered much toil and
need."

Part 2: The Course of the War

Letter from Jerónimo López

The following letter from Jerónimo López to the emperor Charles V
describes the beginnings of the war, although not entirely accurately.
López did not participate in the campaign to suppress the uprising.
He was a prominent figure in Mexico City who often provided the
king with his opinion on affairs in New Spain. He went with Francisco Cortés to Nueva Galicia in 1524, which may account for his
interest in and knowledge of the region. He claimed to have written
an account of that expedition, which he gave to its sponsor, Hernando
Cortés. If that was true it might have been the only fairly complete
narrative of events, but unfortunately it has not been found.[10]

9. Ibid.
10. No. 39, legajo 22, Diversos Colecciones, Archivo Histórico Nacional, Madrid.
Transcribed in "Relacion de la Conquista de Nueva Galicia, alzose año de 1542: Anónima tercera," in Razo Zaragoza, *Crónicas de la Conquista*, 329–43.

First of all, it should be known that the origin of the uprising in this province [Nueva Galicia] was not giving the tributes [that] the Indians owed to certain lords of pueblos [encomenderos] who in that province live, especially those who live in the towns of Guadalajara and Compostela. . . .

The first pueblos that rose up were Suchipila [Juchipila] and Apozol and Xalpa and other neighboring pueblos because this is the principal place, being as its people are Cazcanes and Chichimecas and the most powerful there are in that province. These pueblos and their people left their houses and the fields they had and went to the heights of the mountains, which in the language of the Indians are called *peñoles*. The first of the said peñoles was Mixton[11] and the second Nochistlan and the third Acatique and the fourth Coyna, and there were many other peñoles, but at the time that the *adelantado* [Pedro de Alvarado] and other Spaniards came, there remained only these four peñoles, in which they built forts until it became known by the vecinos of Guadalajara and Compostela. Wanting to resolve the situation, the captain named Cristóbal de Oñate, who was acting as lieutenant governor for Francisco Vázquez de Coronado, assembled up to forty horsemen and an equal number of footmen and some peaceful Indians. They departed from the town of Guadalajara and went to the first peñol, which was Mixton. Trying to bring them in peace, he made all the necessary Requirements, and also interpreters went, so they received Requirements from friars as well as other interpreters, and with little fear of God they killed a Franciscan friar.[12] Not content with that, assuring the Christians that they wished to come in peace, one morning at 4 a.m. they came down from the mountain, or peñol, some 15,000 Indians, naked and with bows and arrows and hair down to their waist and on their right leg hose made of the pelt of a dog, and in this fashion they attacked the Christians so vigorously that they were forced to abandon

11. López is incorrect about this, as in a number of other respects. Mixton probably became the largest of the fortified strongholds over the course of the war, especially because defenders of others took refuge there when they were defeated, but it was not the first established nor was it the first that the Spaniards discovered.

12. Here López conflated events. There was one well-known incident in which a friar was slain, but it probably occurred before Oñate's unsuccessful attack on Mixton.

the field, and they lost some of their people [as well as] many of the Indian allies they had brought with them, and they also killed all the blacks that the said captain Cristóbal de Oñate brought with him. From there they [the Spaniards] retreated to Guadalajara and from there sent notice to the viceroy of certain towns of Spaniards, namely Michoacan, Colima, Zacatula, La Purificación, Compostela, and other pueblos in which there were Spaniards who served as interpreters, who knowing their great need collected up to 150 horsemen, among them the captains Juan de Alvarado, don Luis de Castilla, Cristóbal de Oñate, and other highly placed individuals who left their houses and estates to go to help. They all gathered in Guadalajara, and while they were there, perhaps for two weeks, they learned from other friendly Indians how Tenamaztle and don Francisco, the lords of Nochistlan, and many other pueblos had united to attack the town of Guadalajara. Fearing that they had few people, the Christians sent notice to the *adelantado* don Pedro de Alvarado, the governor of Guatemala, who was in the Pueblos de Ávalos that are about eighteen or twenty leagues from Guatemala toward the southern sea [the Pacific] and was waiting for the opportunity to embark for the Moluccan Islands, which are in the said sea. The *adelantado*, knowing the great necessity of the Christians, having [received] notice that the Indians who were coming were numerous, took all the people who were about to embark, both horsemen and footmen who were altogether around 100 men, and they departed and passed through the canyon of Tonala in one day and a night, although the route through which they passed cannot [normally] be crossed in three days because just to cross the ravine takes a day because it is very rough and also because of the river and the ruggedness of the mountain. The entire shore of this river and ravine is populated by Indians called Zacatecas, who are great archers. [But] at this time when the *adelantado* passed through, they had not risen because they were subject to Tonala until they heard of the death of the *adelantado*. . . .[13]

---

13. It is highly unlikely that there were Zacateca Indians living in the area he describes. Far from being subject to Tonala, the Zacatecas were an independent group living north of Cazcan territory. López, however, was correct in suggesting that the

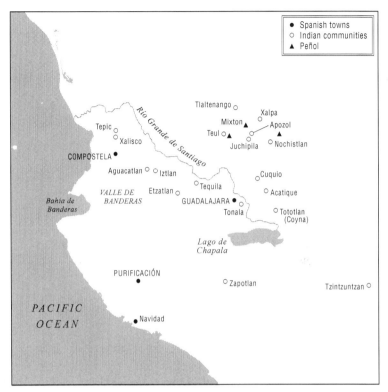

MAP 4 Main sites of the Mixton War

The battle turned into a rout for the Spaniards, and Pedro de Alvarado suffered mortal injuries when his horse slipped during the retreat and another man's horse fell on top of him. He was carried to Guadalajara, where he died a few days later. Spanish horsemen subsequently managed to fend off a massed indigenous attack on the city, but the tide of the war turned decisively in favor of the Spaniards only when the viceroy of New Spain, don Antonio de Mendoza, led a major expeditionary force from central Mexico into the west, recruiting thousands of native troops there and in Michoacan,

---

news of Pedro de Alvarado's death, by demonstrating the Spaniards' fallibility, very likely encouraged communities that up to that point had not joined the insurrection to do so. The coalition fighting the Spaniards expanded to include groups other than the Cazcanes.

as Nuño de Guzmán had done ten years before.[14] The arrival of this massive force soon gave the Spaniards a decisive advantage, and they were able to overwhelm one indigenous stronghold after another.

Account of Don Francisco de Sandoval Acacitli

One of the most interesting accounts of the Mixton War is that of don Francisco de Sandoval Acacitli, the indigenous ruler of Tlalmanalco in Chalco, near Mexico City, who participated in the viceroy Mendoza's campaign against the western rebels.[15] Don Francisco had his account set down in Nahuatl by Gabriel de Castañeda, who identified himself as *principal* (noble) and native of the Barrio de Mechoacan Colomochoco. It was translated into Spanish in 1641 by Pedro Vásquez, an interpreter for the audiencia, and the Nahuatl original subsequently was lost.[16]

The account covers six months of the campaign and is by far the most detailed narrative provided by any participant in the conflict. Although his observations were limited to his immediate experiences, don Francisco's perspective as one of Mendoza's indigenous allies is unique. It provides information on the labor performed by the allies and their role in the fighting as well as insights into the relationships that Mendoza forged with the indigenous rulers who fought with him. In this account the people of western New Spain are called Chichimecas, with little distinction made among the ethnic groups. All the lords or rulers, including don Francisco, as well as the viceroy Mendoza, are called *señor*. Typical of accounts in this period, the narrative voice shifts from first to third person, sometimes in the same sentence. As a result, at times it is unclear who is the subject, and

14. For a comparison of Guzmán's and Mendoza's treatment of their indigenous allies during their respective campaigns, see Altman, "Conquest, Conversion, and Collaboration," in Matthew and Oudjik, *Indian Conquistadors*, 145–74. As seen in this account, Viceroy Mendoza treated the indigenous leaders as his willing allies, not his minions (as had Guzmán). The indigenous forces fared far better under Mendoza's command than they did during Guzmán's entrada, from which almost none returned to central Mexico.

15. Don Francisco de Sandoval Acacitli (or Acazitzin) allied with the Spaniards during the conquest and probably as a result was baptized and recognized by Hernando Cortés as ruler of Tlalmanalco (*tlatqui teuhctli*) around 1521. He remained as ruler until 1554. See Schroeder, *Chimalpahin*, 92, 98.

16. My translation is based on Sandoval Acacictli, *Conquista y pacificación*.

the account can be difficult to understand in parts. This translation is intended to reflect the character of the narrative and does not attempt to resolve all its ambiguities.

When he went to the war of the Chichimecas, don Francisco Acacitli carried for his insignia and arms a feathered face-covering with green plumes, a shield of the same with a center of worked gold, his sword, and his cloak, and [he was] dressed in a red doublet, breeches, shoes and half boots, a great white hat and large kerchief tied around his head, and a necklace of stones with two chains. They left on this march on Monday, the day of San Miguel Archangel, the twenty-ninth of September in the year of the birth of our lord 1541.

I, don Francisco de Sandoval, cacique and señor that I am of this city of San Luis Tlalmanalco, having learned [from] the lord viceroy don Antonio de Mendoza, who lives in the great city of Mexico, and the royal audiencia that there was a war in the land of the Chichimecas of Xuchipila, I went to the said city and entreated the lord viceroy that he would grant me the favor that I would go with the people of my province of Chalco to serve in this war, like Amenecan, Tenango, Xochimilco, and those from here in Tlalmanalco, and all with good will agreed to go to serve in the said war, including the principal people of the republic, as the military and the leaders of it. And I, the said don Francisco, provided for the said war my two sons, who were named don Bernardino del Castillo and don Pedro de Alvarado, who at the time obeyed me, and I gave them arms of Ychehuipil,[17] shields, and swords. It being time to leave for the said war, all of us from Tlalmanalco then made a muster and review of all the people and arms that were provided for this, coming out in person I, don Francisco de Sandoval, and don Fernando de Guzmán and all the principal men, officials of the republic and leaders, and all the rest of the common people, the said muster being made [on] the Sunday, which was the time that we left here from Tlalmanalco.

---

17. Possibly *ichcahuipilli*, body armor of quilted cotton; see Hassig, *Aztec Warfare*, 270.

We left Monday and slept in Mexicatzinco, and then we were in Mexico [City] for two days and left there Thursday, then we slept in Itispapaltetitlan, and then we went to Toluca, where we were for three days, Friday, Saturday, and Sunday. From there we left on Monday, and we slept in Metztepec and left Tuesday, slept in Tlatzacatepec, left Wednesday and went to spend the night in Xuitlan, and from there left on Thursday and slept in Huilacatlan, and from there the cacique don Fernando de la Cerda left because he had gotten sick from a bloody flux. . . .

[A week later they reached the shore of what he called the Chicucxeahuatl River.]

We were there four days. On Monday we were busy making rafts [to place] on canoes in order to cross the said river, where the natives suffered danger and some were carried away by the river. On Tuesday the bridge was finished, over which all the people passed; Wednesday and Thursday they were there; Friday we left there and slept in a valley. We arrived provided with our arms, and at night there were sentinels and guards.

Saturday we left and slept in Tecpaiocan and then on Sunday in Totolan, which was won when the people of Chalco arrived and they were fighting, because on the upper part there were seven barricades that had been won and on the lower part just one, with which they were winning the battle, and the viceroy was on the lower part. The señor don Francisco began to climb up at the same time the viceroy did, and he called to don Francisco and said to him, well, don Francisco, was it well done? And he responded, very well, lord, you have done the job. And the viceroy responded, the people of Chalco are very good. The battle began in the evening, and they were defeated at sunset. Monday we were there; Tuesday we left and went to stay on the edge of the woods; Wednesday we left and arrived at Acatlan, where we were for four days. Thursday and Friday were quiet, and Saturday it was intended to give battle [so] on Friday they went to place the artillery on some rocks where Spaniards and natives stood guard, and at night they said from where the Spaniards were don't shoot your artillery any more so as to frighten the people of the pueblo. In the morning they will go to see the Spaniards.

At dawn they began to march, Maldonado[18] leaving first and
taking with him the señor don Francisco, and they went to meet
up with the Spaniards who were acting as spies. From there
they returned and came to tell the viceroy that they wanted to
advance, and he said no, that they once again should pursue,
and then they left and having arrived at the edge of the rocks,
they began to open the way and left a space where Maldonado stopped and began to call to the Chichimecas through an
interpreter, saying to them, come out and come, and they did
not answer. And then after a while he told don Francisco, you
call them, and he began to shout to them, and then together
they went down to the barricade, where they stopped. Then
señor don Francisco began to descend, and he also stopped at
the incline. And then Maldonado said to him, don't go down,
don Francisco, also that *principal* should go, and then Juan Tza-
uhiutsintle descended and a *criado*[19] of Maldonado, so they too
went to stop on the incline. Then Maldonado said, don Francisco
go down and call to them. He went down and found them in the
water without shields or swords [*macanas*] and began to call
them, saying to them don't be afraid, that the viceroy is calling
you and those of your people, and from fear they did not want
[to come], and he was talking to them for a long while. And
the señor drank water and started again to persuade them until
they wanted to come, and then two of the Chichimecas crossed
the river, one of them named Diego and the other was not yet
baptized and both were interpreters. And they ascended with the
señor guiding them. And then Maldonado, as they were quarrel-
ing, asked them where was the señora, and they answered that
she had gone up to see the señor viceroy, and then he said it was
well done and went to bring hens, eggs, and food, and then they
went to stop at the hill. Then Maldonado told Diego Hernández,
you go for them, and he went and brought them, and Pedro
Hernández had gone with the señor when he went down to the
water, and then Maldonado said, come here, you need to go see
the viceroy. Then he called Pedro Hernández, Martín de Silva,
and Gabriel de Castañeda and told them to escort him. They

18. Maldonado was one of Mendoza's captains.
19. In this case it is not possible to know if the criado was Spanish or indigenous.

went up and, having arrived in the señor viceroy's presence, he asked the interpreter, saying, where is don Francisco, and he told him that he had gone to Nochtian [Nochistlan], and then he [Maldonado?] told him to go for maize. The viceroy called Pedro Hernández and Martín de Silva and Gabriel de Castañeda and said, go with him, and he also made a Spaniard go with them and then they descended. Silva could not descend, and Captain Miguel de Guevara went to bring from there a horse, saddle, and sword, which he brought to the presence of the viceroy. Then they came to see him, and he ordered them that they should destroy their barricades and burn their huts.

We left here on Monday and slept on the mountain, and Tuesday we left here on the plain by the water. Wednesday we departed and went to sleep at Yepcalco, where the hot water is, and there was a great crush [of people] and some were pushed off the rocks, and a great river with salt beds on its banks was passed. We left here Thursday and slept at Misquititlan [Mezquitutan], and then they went to account for those who were there and they all crossed. And only the viceroy with all the Spaniards went ahead and all the natives remained. Only three lords went with the viceroy, who were don Francisco, he of Tlalmanalco, and don Juan of Coyoacan and don Mateo of Cuitlahuac, and they went to take a walk and reconnoiter the hill where the enemies were. And in the place where the entire army of natives stopped, they began to provide themselves with arms and to march, and they went below to stop, where they were met by the captain of Tlacotlan, who brought with him those of Tonallan, and [there] went with them Martín de Silva and Esteban of Xochimilco, who had taken the sick people to Tonallan were with them. And for those who were wounded in Totolan as well as those who had fallen sick leaving Acatlan at that time, [he] did nothing, other than he put the people in order. The next day [was] Saturday, and they began to pursue and nothing could be done. They shot arrows and fired at some. We were there no more than four days—Sunday, Monday, Tuesday and Wednesday, which was the fifth day on which the battle began in the morning around the time that Mass is celebrated. And the order that they had for the battle and combat was that the artillery was placed in the middle, and on one side

of the road went the Tlaxcaltecas, Huejotzincas, Quauquechul-
tecas, and then followed the Mexicanos and Xilotepecas and
then the Aculhuas; and on the other side those of Michoacan,
Mestitlan, and the Chalcas, and they went positioning the
artillery toward the wooden barricade and then the stone one,
at which the Chichimecas abandoned them. The señor don
Francisco, with his device of Quetzapatzactli of green plumes,
[went] after them, by which they gained the barricade and
broke it and burned their shacks and began to fight with them,
with which they left most of their barricades that they had on
the steep hill, which they defended strongly, which was the last
barricade in front of their houses. And the royal standard with
which they were defeated ascended, and they began to capture
them, and some of our [people] fell from the rocks with their
captives. And it was there that all those from the provinces had
many captives,[20] and no more than four Spaniards died in the
battle. The combat continued until this pueblo of Nochistlan
was defeated.

We were there four days, Thursday, Friday, Saturday, and
Sunday, and from there the province of Chalco took charge of
carrying the artillery, pulling or dragging it, by which their
work was doubled, and they also carried on their backs all the
ammunition and equipment for it and the care of the sheep.
Monday we left for Juchipila and went to spend the night on
the edge of another mountain. We left here on Wednesday and
arrived at Juchipila, where the enemy had their camp. The next
day, Thursday, Maldonado, with don Francisco following, went
where they were, which is named Listonco and Tlanoselos to
those of the province of Chalco.

Going very early in the morning Maldonado and don Francisco, with all his people, passed through Ahuizolco and then
began to ascend and pass a small hill and then a small mountain, and then he went down and in the middle met up with the
Mexicanos. They said to him, señor, where are you going, now
that the Chichimecas are coming? And the señor did not pay it

---

20. The viceroy's decision to allow his Indian allies to take most of the captives
after the fall of the peñol of Nochistlan was controversial. He defended his decision by
saying that his allies should receive some reward for their efforts.

any attention and went along with them, and then again went
to meet with another Amecamecan, who spoke the same argu-
ments: señor, where are you going, now that the Chichimecas
are coming? Having walked very little, as he now was reaching
the river, he returned. And of the Chichimecas, part of them
came retreating toward our [forces], and the other part were
going up to try to overtake us, from where they were forced
back from where the señor had them and nobody passed. The
last to come was Maldonado and Salinas, who carried the royal
standard, and only one of the people from Tenantzinco died,
a vassal of Maldonado. And the next morning, which was
Friday, once again the two captains, which were the same Maldonado and the captain from Tlacotlan, went again and again
forced them to withdraw, and they did not take with them
any natives. And they shot the captain from Tlacotlan with an
arrow in the leg and another in the hand, and also shot three
horses with arrows.

The following day, Saturday, the viceroy went [with] all the
Spaniards [but] he took only the Mexicanos. Their leaders were
Tapia and don Martín from Tlatelolco. At night the viceroy
took over the position of the Mexicanos, and the Mexicanos
being in front of the Spaniards, and behind them were posi-
tioned the Mexicanos and part of the Spaniards. They slept in
Apozolco, and they went now in daylight, and they wanted to
advance, and the viceroy was silent and the Mexicanos in their
positions. Having reached the river, they began to call to them,
and they answered, tomorrow we will go to see the señor. And
then they came and brought the viceroy, and the whole army of
natives came, and the next day [was] Sunday.

As the sun went down behind the mountains, the enemies
came out who wanted to attack us at night, and the Chichimecas came down to the foot of the mountain where we were. And
in the lead were the people of Chalco and those of Quahuatitlan
and Coyoacan and Xilotepec, and the other at the position of
the Chalcas, who defended their position very well, and they
almost captured the señor don Francisco, because he attacked
two, armed only with an old shield without a sword. Then he
armed himself with his Ycachihuipil and with his shield and
sword and other devices and then strongly engaged with the

Chichimecas so that they did not dare return again. Seven of them died and two were captured alive, whom the viceroy saw and questioned, and they did not want to say anything. On the third day, which was Wednesday, he beat them, and the Spanish people were counted and on Friday those of the infantry, which were the musketeers and crossbowmen.

We saw at the summit of the sierra of Xuchipiltepetl [peñol of Juchipila] that there was a very large temple of the devil, and Montezopo was there, and the room was fifteen *brazas* [measurement of about two yards] long and three wide, and the walls were all of stone like the adobe of a very old building, and no one knows who built it. The hill was the base of the building with all the hollows [formed by] the rocks in very rough and difficult places. The people who lived there, all their houses were of very pretty flagstones. . . . This type of stone is like that which is mined at Senoc, and part of the exterior was of stone, and the shape of the hill is circled by a river so that it seems that the water comes out of the hollows in the rocks, and the current is very wide. There are four paths by which to go up, of which there are four that circle the rocks, at times very steep and difficult.

We left marching on Sunday toward the hill and slept at the foot of the hill of Mixtepec, where they went to prepare, and we went to sleep in Apozolco. Then on Monday we left here and went to sleep at the foot of the same hill of Mixtepec, and when we arrived the enemies were in sight but not making any noise or shouting. On Tuesday we began to march, and we came to some large rocks while descending and with a very narrow passage, and the trail by which we went was a ridge with both sides of split rock. And having gone down by the rocks and marching underneath a great boulder, the Chichimecas intended to take the army, and from the top of the said boulder they began to roll great rocks and hurled them at our people, and threw [them] at our [people], whence they flung them. And some of them were captured and others wounded, and fighting fiercely they were followed to the river, where they were overtaken. The enemies strongly defended the pass and by pure force [were] thrown out of the river, and they were followed to the slope, our people fighting from above and below, and there we spent the night at the edge of the ravine, in which there was a great rock, under which the viceroy slept and near where we were confronting the Chichimecas.

We proceeded on Wednesday and descended a very steep ravine that in part was very rough and dangerous, and the people were very crowded, some [climbing] over others who were going up the rocks. The priests and a captain who went with them went ahead along with some harquebusiers and thus arrived at their wall. Nearby they gave a single shout that they were there near the said house, and then one of the priests began to call to them, saying, come here, sons, it is possible that you do not have pity for your wretched selves, but you should know that we love you very much, and the lord viceroy also loves you greatly; come here to see him. They did not respond and remained silent, and they were calling them for a good while. And also they [tried to] persuade them to give them some of the native soldiers, saying to them, Xuchipiltecas come here, and your interpreter should come, that the priests are calling you [in order] to tell the truth; if you are resolved that we should give battle, respond. None of them replied, and below they began to fight again, and behind them was where one of the captains was, who was Maldonado.

The Chichimecas understood that they had been caught unprepared and that there were no guards, and they were chased off. And they [the Spaniards' allies] suffered greatly in moving the artillery, because the native soldiers carried them between many rocks until crossing the river, where they turned to return. And regarding that they mistreated the nobles (*principales*) who were forced to go back to meet up with the Tlax-caltecas at a place when it already was nightfall, and they went down the river to where they left them and from there the people of Michoacan took charge of it [the artillery], as well as people from other provinces. And we the Chalcas began to exert ourselves to move our loads because we were ascending a very large and rocky mountain, and our soldiers and even our leaders suffered great toil without exception because everyone was dragging the artillery. And the señor had gone ahead and had arrived to where we quartered the first time, and from there they returned, taking with them the interpreter Antonio Ortiz.

And from there finally they went to meet the artillery, and the sun already had gone down when they reached them, and they arrived with it already past nightfall, where they slept as they had continued dragging [lighting their way] with torches. What the Tlaxcaltecas were carrying they could not reach there with it and so slept with it on the slope, and the next morning arrived with it.

On Thursday they rested and began a seven days' march on Friday, and on the eighth day they reached and destroyed the enemies. This was so sudden, because the señor viceroy had not given the order of how they would conduct the battle. This occurred on Thursday, the eighth day of the Conception, because they were working and building, and there were not many who fought other than some companies, because they were not all armed or provisioned to go into battle. The Spaniards also were unprepared when it happened, which was around evening time, and so suddenly that it was a miracle from God in the way it occurred. There were no captives made prisoners, . . . and very few deaths because all the others fled. The order that they had for this march was that the Mexicanos were responsible for clearing the part below with all those of their group who are called of the Chinampa, and above, over the rocks, was the most difficult part, which was a narrow passageway in which only one person could fit in order to go through it, and that these devices and the manner in which one had to work in it. The people of Michoacan went first, and then the Chalcas followed, because the rock continued, and it was necessary to construct a bridge of beams and break some large rocks and to dig them [out] so they could destroy them. And they followed the Tlaxcaltecas and Huejotzincas. Where they worked they filled an opening in a large boulder with earth and stone, and at the end of the rocks the artillery was placed and in the back of it they placed a wall of stone with four posts and in front of it an enclosure made of wood. They covered it with earth in the part where they fired the shots from the artillery and where the viceroy was, and on the other part that was the slope toward the east were those who cleared the path.

At the time that they won on another day, which was Friday, Maldonado went to Xalpan and took señor don Francisco.

We slept on the bank of the river, and then on Saturday we arrived and some Chichimecas were seized, and they cut off their hands. They also took two women and cut off their breasts. Then Maldonado sent for them and said, go, and call for the señor that he should come, that if he did not want to come [and] that they had no fear of the Spaniards, they should come. Then they went and all the houses were burned. There was a church that the Chichimecas had destroyed, and there the señor [don Francisco] suffered greatly because he had nothing but toasted maize for supper, and he had no clothes because he brought only his arms and a thin blanket called Yczotil-mantli. He slept armed in his Huichahuipil, and all the rest of the people also suffered greatly because they all were without clothes or food. They came to sleep again on the bank of the river near some rocks, which was Saturday, and Sunday we arrived on the mountain where the people were.

And we were on the mountain twelve days, and before the Monday on which they were to leave there they killed twelve of the Chichimecas with a shot from a piece of artillery that killed them, taking off their heads and other parts of their body, and another an arm and a head, making pieces of their bodies as if in a whirlwind, and their hands and flesh fell on the people. And some of it remained in the trees, and on the high mountain where they were encamped they hanged seventeen and another seventeen they shot, and they stoned five, and another six were hanged at the place where the viceroy was. At the top of the mountain they cut down all the trees and destroyed it and laid waste to all their enclosures.

On Tuesday all the people were divided there, on one side the viceroy went with all the captains and lords of the provinces and Maldonado. We left there and came to sleep in Apozolco. The artillery took two days to arrive because we had left the artillery there. The Tlaxcaltecas dragged two pieces and the Mexicanos one and another the Tepanecas, who brought them as far as Tonallan. What happened at Apozolco was that they overtook all the people so they would not come because there were many who were coming with those who were hauling the artillery. So little by little the Tlaxcaltecas left, and the next day the Mexicanos and Zapotecas, and they left in the presence of

Maldonado and don Luis del Castillo [don Luis de Castilla] who was in charge of the artillery, and everyone else in the army wanted to come so they would not be overtaken at night. There were sentinels and guards so that no one would leave from there. We were there two days, which were Wednesday and Thursday.

On Friday we left for Xalpan, and as soon as we arrived fifteen Chichimeca men were captured, and an inquiry was made to them regarding the señor and other natives and vassals. None of them replied; rather, they showed fear. One of them spoke and said where the señor and the rest of the vassals were, and on Saturday he sent two of them along with the interpreters, one of them a native of Tonala and the other of Apozolco named Tepocicatl, and a Spaniard. And then they brought them. The señor was named don Pedro and with him [came] three nobles and three commoners, and they asked him, where have you been? He replied that he had been in the woods. They asked him again about the other people, and don Pedro responded that they had scattered, with two in some places and three in others. They replied that he should order all the people to come and not to be afraid, that they would not be killed. He pleaded on their behalf with the viceroy that he not order them killed because he loved them very much. By not coming, and there having come all the sons of the provinces, because if they were to look for them they would all be made slaves and consider the great number of people who had been brought just for this purpose. Then don Pedro responded that it was fortunate, that he would send for them, and that he knew that nearby there were three lords, but he did not know where his lady the queen was, that they would look for her. This was ordered Saturday evening, and the next day don Pedro came with his mother, who was elderly, and another woman.

Sunday was the day of the Nativity of Our Lord Jesus Christ, and the people went to a meadow in a place named Pitzasco. The reason they went to the meadow, or savannah, was because all the houses were burned. They gave to Maldonado fish, quail, and food for the horses, and on the day of the festival of Our Lord Jesus Christ the people from Amecamecan had their dance. On the third day of Christmas (Pascua), which was Tuesday, the day of Saint John, don Francisco danced and the Chichimeca song was sung. There were flowers and incense, food and cacao drink that they gave to all the lords. All the nations of the different provinces danced with their arms, shields, and swords; everyone danced without exception.

And where we were was called Tlacho, beneath a hill named Quahuitepetl, and on the other side, Xalpan. Maldonado also was given food and drink and flowers and incense. Don Pedro went to visit señor don Francisco, and he gave him one of his shirts, and don Pedro brought him fish, and they became great friends. There the viceroy reached us on Saturday and there heard Mass on Sunday, which was the day of the circumcision of the Lord, when he was named Our Lord Jesus Christ. On Saturday don Pedro went out to receive the viceroy, and they gave him quail, fish, and food for the horses. Four people were hanged in Tlacho. Monday we left there and went to spend the night in Apozolco and were there an entire day. The people of Apozolco came down, and the viceroy was merciful with them and hanged two. On Tuesday all day they pulled up magueys and cut mesquites, and they went by night to Xalpan, only we the Chalcas. Fifteen Spaniards and sixty natives went for this, and twenty were captured. They went to bring the queen, or lady named doña Luisa, and there in Xuchipila came to overtake [her?].

We left on Wednesday and spent the night in Xuchipila, and we stayed there two days. After we arrived the Tlaxcaltecas and Mexicanos began to pull up magueys. At night they arrived with the queen, or lady named doña Luisa, with two women who were with her and an old man, and they went to bring her to Nahuapan. On the next day, which was Thursday, they made forays in all directions, but only in Mixquitonco did they take captives. All those of the provinces had prisoners. When they came they showed the captives they had, and he began to question them so they would say where the Chichimecas were, but they did not explain anything. The viceroy gave to the people of Mixquitonco a document so they would bring their lord, and they were bringing him, but through carelessness he fled from them, and they brought only the interpreter. The viceroy showed him mercy and they surrendered. He ordered that they

gather and hanged four of them, three below and one at the
upper part near the queen, or lady. Then we went to inform
Maldonado, and he came to where señor don Francisco was.
He came for her and gave clothing to her and her daughter and
an old woman and the old man and to another daughter of hers.
Then Maldonado took her for himself to his lodging or quarters
and afterward took her to the presence of the viceroy. He asked
her where she had been, and she answered, in the mountains,
and he replied, the people where were they? She responded
that they had all scattered. The viceroy said, all is well, since
you are a woman. If you were a man I would hang you, so go
and gather your vassals and do not join the Xuchipiltecas.
Whoever comes of them you should order to kill, and if some
come together, if you want to congregate them, go then to warn
Mexico in order that the Spaniards come to kill them. Then don
Pedro of Xalpa went with her, and after that they pulled up the
magueys and cut the mesquites. On Friday, which was the Day
of Kings [January 6], nothing was done.

On Saturday morning we left. At the foot of the hill they
overtook us because they had learned that we had to come
there heading for Tonallan. There the señor inspector divided
us up, and another captain took the Texcocanos. The viceroy
went in the middle of those from Mexico, Tlaxcala, and Chalco;
we went with him, and another captain named Bocanegra
went behind the hill through the woods where the viceroy
went. He went up; it was a very dangerous and rough part,
and we went to sleep in Miahuatlan, where we went as we left.
We began to go up a very high mountain, and emerging at the
top of it we traveled a little on a good plain and then began to
go down through a very dangerous part because the mountain
was very high. There a Spaniard died, who fell on his horse,
injuring himself greatly. Many of the natives rolled [down].
Beneath the mountain the river passes. There the viceroy ate
hearts of palm together with all the rest of the Spaniards and
natives, and don Francisco ate the same and all the nobles, and
with that they sustained themselves there all day, at the place
where we saw the hot water. On Monday we began to march
and slept at the foot of a hill in a ravine, and there again the
señor don Francisco ate hearts of palm and so did all the nobles

and natives and the Spaniards the same, so that it was two days
that they lived on hearts of palm.

On Tuesday we left and went to spend the night at Tepanca,
and we left at dawn to ascend the mountain, which was very
rocky. Having come out at the top, we began to descend, and
when we reached the houses everyone already had fled, and
we went after them. Some of those who were captured were
by the hands of those who followed, and the Chichimecas who
were [captured] it was in ravines and in the roughest parts of
the rocks. No one was found in the houses. There at the end of
the ravine they were overtaken, and there the lord of Tepanca
was taken to the presence of the viceroy. The Spaniards in
the mountain went to bring them, and he brought a basket of
tamales and fish that he gave to the viceroy, and he brought
with them eight Chichimecas, who slept in chains. It was not
clear whether they came in peace or if they deceived the viceroy. The next day, which was Wednesday, they began looking
for them. They went to collect them in very dangerous places
between ravines and boulders and brambles. Looking for and
pursuing them lasted five days and all five days capturing them.
On Sunday after vespers they hanged the lord of Tepanca on
the bank of the Río Tunhuamuchitl and from the rest took
their statements so they would say where the Chichimecas
were, and from fear they told it [to them]. It was in vain that
they took them to show [them], and wherever they took them
they hanged them there because they did not find anyone.
Where they had their settlements they overran everything in
two days, and those who came from behind the mountain once
again met up with those who went from here. Those who went
from here the other way, toward Mistinco, which was how the
inspector and Miguel de Guevara, chief captain of Tlacotlan,
went. They took many Chichimecas, rounding them up in their
houses. . . .

[After a few days of fighting they traveled along the river,
which was very deep in some places and proved treacherous.]

On Monday we left, and not very far from here we went
[to find] where to sleep, and they went on two routes, so that
those who walked on the banks of the river forded it three
times, and those who went on the upper part forded it once.

There some of them were lost and went directly to the mountain, and others went down to the river, where they spent the night, and there they were drowned, and the river carried them away because it had [great] depth, in parts reaching their chests, in parts the waist, in parts less and in parts more. On Sunday the sheep and cattle passed, and also many natives, and the river even carried away one of the Spaniards, who escaped and did not die. And in Tepanca they absented themselves and don Diego Quataxochitl and his older brother Martín Quaxolocatl came. They went to sleep at night and did not rise, the Quataxochitl being the younger brother of señor don Fernando, and Martín Quaxolocatl the older brother of the said don Fernando.

Then on Wednesday we left and went to spend the night at Copalla, ascending at a very steep place. As soon as we got going, we began to ascend among boulders, and we all went the same way, including those on horseback. The natives suffered much toil in this ascent. One from the Otomi nation died when a horse fell on him and cut off his legs, and the horse died. The natives also went ascending, always between rocks, where some went after others. They stopped there a good deal because of finding themselves overtaken. The señor don Francisco ascended between rocks, and there toward the middle of the ascent it was necessary to go up over a bramble or reeds.

On Thursday we left and went to spend the night in Teccistlan and were there all day Friday. There the señor gave chili and salt to those of Chalco; they gave us a mat and two cakes of salt. Some of the Spaniards turned around, and many of the natives fled. And those who were taken at Tepanca were branded there, and in Teccistlan the viceroy and inspector Bocanegra reached [us]. Many took their leave, and the viceroy did not want it. And he responded that it remained only to follow him and that they would go to Mexico. There the Tlaxcaltecas left, and the viceroy said, well done, go as you did with the *marqués*,[21] whom you abandoned, and once again you do the same with me in leaving before the war is finished. What news will you take there? Enough already, from here on do not boast of being good soldiers or of having gone to conquests. And the

21. The *marqués* mentioned here is the Marqués del Valle, or Hernando Cortés.

Mexicanos, although at one time they were our rivals before they belonged to the emperor,[22] now attend scrupulously to the things for which they are obligated until reaching the end of it. So go, and although you say that you want to go with me, it is not my desire. And apart from that all the equipment of the viceroy remained there, and the people of Huejotzinco were charged with taking it to Tonallan. Also departed the carts of the Spaniards, which also were taken to Tonallan, and parts of these loads were taken here. And the hunger started in Teccistlan, and there they sold their clothes and outfits. Saturday we left and went to sleep on the mountain that was above, and the ridge there was like sand.

We left on Sunday and went to spend the night in Tequila near the houses. There we experienced great thirst, and it was necessary to finish the water since the maize that the señor ate also was finished. And there the people of San Juan helped us with a large basket of maize and a bowl of fruit, or rather beans, which he ate in two days, and on the third there was enough only for lunch, and it was from there that the Tlaxcaltecas returned.

On Thursday we left and got to Tequila, and after we were there a day the viceroy sent people of Tequila and Etzateca, giving them papers and [the] order in which to bring them. The next day he sent someone to bring the Etzatecas, and they slept there, and the next day they returned when the viceroy wanted to march. A lord named don Alonso came, and the viceroy said to the Etzatecas, you have done very well in having brought them. Then he commanded the Tequiltecas, [saying] because now the señor has pity he will show mercy toward you. Come out from wherever you are and do not go back there; let all the people come out. And they answered him that they would do so, and they acknowledged the mercy that the señor showed toward them, and the people were put in order.

And on Tuesday there was a dance, and the señor gave us, together with those of Quaquechula, a young bull, and all the natives cooked [it] on a barbecue [with] leaves of maguey, which the Spaniards also ate because there was nothing else to

22. The emperor is Charles V.

sustain themselves. And there the señor received the Etzatecas. . . . And at the time that the señor spoke with them, they
gave him five arrows wrapped in deerskin and told him, here
we bring the deceiver. The señor viceroy began to unwrap them
and then broke them in pieces, and he said, what is this, that
they deceived you into helping [them], that if you shot something with them and you know for certain that you must shoot.
Then he told them many things regarding the holy Catholic
faith. And here also many natives left the army. On Wednesday
we left there and went to spend the night in Nexpa, and as soon
as we left we began to ascend a mountain on the summit of
which all the rocks were very sharp. . . . In front of it there was
a great lake, where we arrived late at night and slept, and others were unable to reach the place because it was a long march.
On that occasion there was nothing for supper except some
toasted maize and *pinoles*[23] that the people of Tlailotlacan gave
them. They did not make huts to sleep in.

On Thursday we left and went to stay the night in Temicie,
and in the morning when we left the señor don Francisco had
nothing to eat but some small [dried?] fruit kneaded between
the hands and the *pinole* that the people of Tlailotlacan gave
him. His horse did not eat maize because there in Tequila he
ate what the people of San Juan gave him, and during the days
that it took to get to Temicie he did not eat anything. We were
there in Temicie Friday and Saturday, and when we arrived
there they made forays looking for maize. From there the Chichimecas observed them and shot at the soldiers with arrows,
including another from Chalco named Bartolomé. On Friday
they went to seek the enemy, who could not be found at hand,
no more than four or five people because they could not be
caught. Where the viceroy was it was a temple that was as high
as the large rocks that looked like statues of people, and in the
middle of them were holes, and on top was a house in which
there were some trees, and below it the river passed. Here the
señor don Francisco began to get sick, which was on Friday. The
viceroy found out and sent for him from there in Etzatlan, saying, go to Etzatlan to wait for me and so that Sancho López will

23. *Pinoles* possibly means pine nuts (*piñones*).

treat you. Señor don Francisco did not want [to go], saying that he wanted to go with the señor viceroy and that God would be served, whether he lived or died, and giving them health because it was all according to his will, and that he would go little by little so that he was sick until reaching Huacatlan [Aguacatlan]. And there in Temicie many natives deserted, and from there Felipe Quahuihuitl of Toscoc [Texcoco?] fled and the captains of Tlailotlacan and Amistlato and others. . . .

[After another couple of days of difficult marching, they reached Aguacatlan to spend the night.]

Where we slept it was a flat valley and having arrived in Aguacatlan, which had settlements in the valley and in the middle of it a river passed, where the people had stopped and built huts. Only the viceroy passed [on] and also with him the captains, and all the natives stopped, not a single one went. But the viceroy went to where the Chichimecas were, which was called Texalatzinco. The *veedor*, who had gone ahead since Ytzlan, which was on the edges of the mountain, came to meet the viceroy and Tapia to bring the army to Texalatzinco, the runners [having] gone ahead and all the loads behind. On this occasion there were not many captives other than some women and children they caught in the large rocks. And he arrived late at night, and where the viceroy made his camp was between two rivers beneath a large stone, and from the interior of the rocks the water burst forth. From where it fell it ran very little because then it sank into the earth. The next day they made forays and some [of the enemy] were caught. In the mountain where they were there was water in some places, and there they grew cotton, chili, tomatoes, avocado trees, and *ají*. All of that mountain or hill was made of sand.

After two days, which was Thursday morning, the Etzatecas brought to the presence of the viceroy two people they had captured, who were questioned so that they would declare where the Chichimecas had gone. And they stated that some of them had gone to the mountains, and others were on the slopes of the hills. Then they went to where they were, the Etzatecas going alone with some Spaniards who went with them, and having seen them they came out to meet them at [the place] where the rocks started and began to fight. And others of the natives of the army, from different pueblos who also had reason, went with them, and having seen them they went out to meet them where the rocks began and started to fight. They were fighting for a very long while, and from there a Spaniard went to summon the viceroy. Already they had run them off and, captured, they were burning their huts and collecting maize, among other spoils. And the Etzatecas caught a horse that the Chichimecas had. The others who were saved were women and men who went up a very large and rocky mountain, the stones very black, and they could not go after them because of the difficulty of the ascent, and they could not pass because the horses could not climb up, even though the viceroy wanted to ascend.

They returned to the middle of the mountain, which is called Tonan and is a volcano that smokes and at the peak has a depression, within which were the Chichimecas. So the viceroy returned without doing anything and arrived at his place when it already was night. The next day was Friday, and two Chichimecas came to him and begged the viceroy that he pardon them; they would come down saying to him, have pity on these people who have suffered much misery and especially the old men and old women. The viceroy said to them that he wished them well, that he loved them, and he also said to them, where is the señor? And they answered that he was there among the rocks. He told them to call him and that he should come the following day. The lord was named don Pedro. And then we ascended the rocks and were there three days—Wednesday, Thursday, and Friday—and there the festival of Santa María that we call the Purificación coincided. On Friday they branded the captives. In Telalatzinco they gave the lord a gourd full of virgin honey, Costlailotlaque. On Saturday morning we left there, and it was not far that we marched because we went to stay the night in Aguacatlan in a corner at the bottom of a hill. Here his illness began to affect señor don Francisco again. In the morning he ate a tortilla kneaded by hand and drank a little water from the river. And wanting to get to where he had to spend the night, he began to be very ill and having arrived began to vomit, which was very painful for him. After we arrived two Chichimecas came to speak with the viceroy, and they told him, we want to come, and our cacique and lord will

not let us come but wants to kill us for it. Many of our natives
have fled, and they were asked how many, and they said, many.
The lord was known as Guzmán. . . .

On Tuesday we left there and went to spend the night in
Etzatlan. Having arrived there the viceroy said farewell to all
the peoples of the many provinces. The lord viceroy said to
them, sons, natives that you are of diverse provinces, go with
best wishes; now the war has finished and come to an end. And
then he ordered that all those who fled and absented themselves should be recorded because he wanted to know them,
that they should be shown in Mexico. And you, having gone in
my company following me, the lords of many places, I hold you
as sons and will favor you in all that arises. Then part of them
came, and others the following day, and those of Tlalmanalco
the viceroy sent first of all that they should come with don
Francisco, and he charged them to go with Maldonado. On this
occasion the lord of that place and a constable [were present].
The viceroy said to them, I esteem and love you greatly in that
here has been the end of the battle. All that you desire I will
give to you, and I shall honor and greatly favor this pueblo.
And so don Francisco you shall have as governor and the constable as *corregidor*.[24] And with that he took his leave of him,
and the señor don Francisco, the lord of Etzatlan, gave him food
to eat and local fowl.

The next day, Wednesday, we left there and came to spend
the night at Ayahualulco, where the viceroy slept as well, and
Maldonado went on a different route that goes toward Tonallan, and everyone else left by the route that came toward Teza-
qualpa. And there in Ayahualulco the señor had lodged, and
there the señor don Francisco did not see those who had come
guarding the loads, and then they went to see to the said loads,
which were Martín Colomuchacatltuitli and Pablo de Sandoval. The señor Maldonado, having found out that señor don
Francisco was not going, he then returned and came for him,

---

24. Spanish authorities were starting to impose their own political arrangements
on indigenous communities. Don Francisco de Sandoval was the ruler of Tlalmanalco,
but at the conclusion of the war Viceroy Mendoza named him governor. He also
appointed a *corregidor*, a Spanish administrator, for the district.

and he was talking with him for a long time. Later they went to bring the people of Amecamecan, Tenango and those of Xochimilco, and Maldonado went to the post to tell the viceroy. Then señor don Francisco went to where he spent the night. Maldonado went in pursuit of him since he ordered that he be found since he had gone, and he took with him the interpreter Ortiz. He only found Antonio Ojeda Achcahutzin, whom he asked about señor don Francisco, [saying] that the viceroy had called for him, because he did not want to go with Maldonado. The viceroy said, call him, that he should come with me, and he answered that he had already left. Then he went, and it was very late at night when Maldonado caught up with us, and he arrived late at night, whereby he went to sleep near where the river passes. Don Francisco went to receive Maldonado with a torch, and both had supper, which ended the relation.

We left Thursday morning and came to spend the night in Ocotla, traveling a good deal and arriving late at night. On Friday we left and went to spend the night at Tonallan, and we were there one day, which was Saturday. There too they gave food to señor don Francisco. He of that place is called Guzmán and don Pedro. On Sunday we heard Mass there and then left, and we went to spend the night in a valley on the shore of a river near two willows. On Monday we left very early in the morning and came to spend the night in Cuixopoian Tijintia, and there found a woman who gave don Francisco some white tortillas. We left on Tuesday and came to spend the night on the shore of a great river, which we crossed by canoe, and the horses they let swim in order to cross them [over], leading them by pulling a canoe. The river was so deep that one could not see the bottom. . . .

We encountered some hot springs. Even before we reached them we saw smoke many times from where they were that rose up greatly. Once we arrived the smoke disappeared, and we saw that where the hot water emerged there was an opening in the rock that was about two *brazas* around on the lower side. When the water wanted to emerge, the rock became whitish and very hot; then suddenly the hot water came out with a great noise and reached a height of more than five *brazas*. There señor don Francisco Maldonado roasted some pieces of pork, which cooked very well in the hot water where it came out. It rose up in five places, all in the same manner, and three [of the five] parts were boiling water, very warm and muddy, and everywhere that it emerges it then disappears and is lost. And there is an evergreen tree and in the manner of a bench another, and when señor don Francisco came to make camp there, the sun was already setting, and when he got up from there it was very little before dawn, and it was late at night where they stopped to sleep. On Friday we left there and went to spend the night at Tlazazalco, all day eating from some mesquites, [and] the sun was setting when we arrived. On Saturday we left and came to Michoacan to sleep. There the trumpeter Tequimotzil came out to receive señor don Francisco de Sandoval and brought him a meal of baked tortillas and other large ones that were dried, cacao ground in pieces and powder, ground *pinole* [as well as] blankets, shirts, trousers, sandals, and footwear that he gave to all the nobles, and we were there also Sunday and Monday, altogether three days. On Tuesday, which was carnival, we went to stay in Teucuitlatlan. There the lord of the pueblo was named don Francisco, and he provided two local fowl and a ham and a large container of wine. The next day, which was Wednesday, we took ash and then began to march. On that same Wednesday we came to spend the night in Tlovacallio in the house of a Spaniard and arrived there while the sun was still up. And there the lord of Michoacan, named don Pedro, gave him food. On Monday we came to spend the night at a mountain, of the sierra Quetzaltepetl. On Friday we left there and came to spend the night in Taximaroa [where] we arrived at vespers. On Saturday we left and stayed at the foot of a very high mountain, Coliuqui, which took us all day to climb. On Sunday we left and came to stay on the slope of a hill called Metlahac and spent all day going down. On Monday we left there and came to spend the night in Tlalchchilco. It was very late when we arrived. We left there on Tuesday and came to sleep in Toluca, where we were all day on Wednesday. There the two lords of Toluca, one named don Luis and the other don Felipe, provided food for señor don Francisco.

We left there on Thursday and got to Acaxuchic, and there señor don Francisco's brother don Pedro Tlacatecultzin came out to greet him. We left there on Friday and came to stay in Mexico [City], where we were for two days, Saturday and Sunday, and did nothing more than say farewell to the señor viceroy don Antonio de Mendoza through the interpreter Antonio Ortiz. Speaking to him, he said, your Illustrious Lordship, I come to kiss your hand and to welcome you on your good return from the journey that your lordship made to the land of the Chichimecas, with such prosperous outcome and without disaster or illness. God has brought you with favor to your house and court in this city of Mexico. Your Illustrious Lordship should rest, as I come to ask permission to go to your pueblo of San Luis Tlalmanalco. And then the interpreter related this to the señor viceroy, and the said interpreter gave his response, saying that his Illustrious Lordship said that I am very grateful to don Francisco and very satisfied with the good that the Chalcas did for the *marqués* [del Valle de Oaxaca] when he came for the conquest and pacification of this kingdom. You helped in all the wars that the *marqués* had, and you should go with congratulations to your house and pueblo of Tlalmanalco to rest. In each and every thing that arises I will do what you ask and favor you.

On Monday we left and spent the night near a pine tree on a plain, and we arrived at night. On Tuesday we left there for this pueblo of Tlalmanalco. The order that they arranged to receive señor don Francisco [was the following]. First a group of the nobles came out to receive him in Tochitltezacuilco; the second was another group [in] Yetlar; [the] third in Osototicpac, with whom don Fernando de Guzmán went and received him there at the place they call Yztompatepec; and Joaquin Tlecomalhua, Cristóbal Maldonado, Bernardino Tlacochchalcatltecutl, and all the rest of the other nobles and ladies, and all around the common people [were there] to receive him. And all along the route there were arches and sedge on both sides [leading] into the interior of the church, and there also were scaffolds from place to place covered in sedge. It was decorated in the same fashion from the church to the palace of don Francisco de Sandoval, and everything was adorned with flowers, with this decoration starting at the pueblo of Yztompatepec. And the said don Fernando made the welcome with all the nobles and headmen and the ladies who on this occasion were here and fray Cristóbal Ruiz as guardian.

Here ends the journey that señor don Francisco made when he went to the conquest and pacification of the pueblos of the Chichimecas here named and declared in this account that has been made.

Don Francisco's account underscores one of the great ironies of the Mixton War. The defeat of western Mexico's autonomous indigenous communities owed a great deal to the participation of indigenous warriors from central Mexico and Michoacan. For leaders like don Francisco de Sandoval Acacitli, the campaign to defeat the uprising in Nueva Galicia represented an opportunity to revive the warrior traditions that the Spanish overthrow of the Aztec Empire had suppressed. The contributions of indigenous fighters from central Mexico were not just symbolic. In addition to playing a crucial role in ensuring Spanish victory, thereby gaining favor with the powerful viceroy, they helped to open the west to the influence of central Mexico in ways that the Aztecs never had achieved. Not only did the diverse peoples of western Mexico pay the price for their defeat in terms of the loss of lives and communities, but after the war they witnessed the arrival of waves of indigenous migrants from central Mexico who came to settle in their midst.

4

Xalisco and the New Order

This chapter focuses on the indigenous province of Xalisco. Because the documentation on Xalisco from Spanish and indigenous sources spans the entire period covered in this volume, it is possible to trace over time the consequences for one community of the imposition of Spanish rule in Nueva Galicia. In particular, rather than showing indigenous-Spanish interactions only in situations of conflict, the records provide a rare glimpse into the more mundane, if not necessarily less violent, experience of the community at the hands of their Spanish overlords. By showing that little changed for the better for this indigenous community after the end of the Mixton War and the introduction of the New Laws, this microhistory of Xalisco can serve as an epilogue to the contested and violent history of the Spanish occupation of Nueva Galicia that is documented here.

The people of Xalisco first came into contact with Spaniards as early as 1524, when the expedition of Francisco Cortés passed through the area. Although that episode entailed some violence, Xalisco apparently formed a short-term alliance with the invading newcomers, possibly under some coercion. As seen in chapter 2, the arrival of Nuño de Guzmán's expedition in 1531 brought much more extensive conflict and destruction to Xalisco and the rest of the region. Men who participated in Guzmán's campaign—and some who did not—received encomiendas, some of which functioned much better than others. Xalisco, one of the more substantial communities, came under the sway of the powerful Cristóbal de Oñate, who was determined to wrest whatever profits he could from its people.

When the native uprising that came to be known as the Mixton War engulfed Nueva Galicia, the people of Xalisco found themselves in a very difficult position. Other pueblos that supported the insurrection pressured the leaders of Xalisco to join them, but probably their ties to Oñate and possible fear of reprisals from the Spanish made them reluctant to rebel. After the war's conclusion the long-suffering people of Xalisco found that sitting out the uprising brought them no rewards, as their relationship to their Spanish overlords scarcely changed.

Following are excerpts from documents that reflect the experiences of the people of Xalisco during a period of about twenty-five years, beginning with the entrada of Francisco Cortés. Much of this composite account is drawn from a volume titled *Xalisco, la voz de un pueblo en el siglo XVI,* which includes documents transcribed from Nahuatl and translated into Spanish by a group of Mexican scholars. The documents date from some time in the sixteenth century and apparently were addressed to, and possibly solicited by, members of the Franciscan order. Eventually, they ended up in the library of the state of Jalisco. The excerpts translated here into English come from an account that appears in the second chapter of the volume.[1] Additional perspectives on Xalisco are drawn from documents from the lawsuit between Nuño de Guzmán and Hernando Cortés, referring in part to the 1524 Francisco Cortés expedition, as well as accounts of Guzmán's expedition and testimony compiled after the conclusion of the Mixton War.

The account from *Xalisco, la voz de un pueblo,* begins as follows.

> Here we would like you to know how another time our lord came ____ our lord don Martín Cortés came here to our home, Xalisco.[2] ____ He did not conquer us; he was received on the road in the field of our lord governor. ____ Then he went to Tepic and later his messenger arrived. . . . Seven people greeted

---

1. Calvo et al., *Xalisco,* 49–108. The document itself appears in Nahuatl and Spanish; my translation is based on the Spanish version. The editors note that parts of the original are in poor condition and that the document incorporates the handwriting of more than one person. Blank spaces (____) indicate places in the text that are missing (parts that apparently were blank, torn, or unreadable in the original document); ellipses indicate parts of the text that I have omitted.

2. The name Martín Cortés must refer to Francisco Cortés.

him, each with a gourd full of gold. _____ There they ordered
that they would keep the tribute of cotton cloth in Colima. . . .³

The description of events here is fairly neutral. Spanish testimony
that was taken in the course of the lawsuit between Hernando Cortés
and Nuño de Guzmán, however, suggests that the people of Xalisco
initially clashed with the Spaniards. Here are the versions of two
Spanish witnesses.⁴

> This witness went with Francisco Cortés _____ and he saw that
> the said Francisco Cortés and the people who went with them
> on the outskirts of Xalisco [were] making war. They went to
> Xalisco, where they were two or three days, and Xalisco made
> peace and they ransomed some Indian men and women who
> had been taken from them. [Testimony of Jerónimo Flores]
>
> This witness went with Francisco Cortés to conquer the
> province of Millpa, and from there they returned to Xalisco,
> and in Xalisco they greeted them with war, and they fought
> with them until they threw them out of the pueblo. Being in
> Xalisco three or four hours thinking they would make peace,
> and they did not, that same day they [the Spaniards] went to
> rest in Tepic, which was one league from there, and the next
> day the people of Xalisco made peace and redeemed the women
> who had been taken. And they went with them and were there
> for three or four days, and then Tepic made peace. And from
> there they went to another pueblo seven leagues from there,
> and all the people of Xalisco and Tepic went with them to help,
> and from that pueblo they [the Spaniards] returned to Colima,
> conquering along the coast. [Testimony of Alonso Quintero]

Another witness in the suit between Hernando Cortés and Nuño
de Guzmán testified as follows regarding the arrival of Guzmán in
1531.

> After they passed some gorges of a large river and reached the
> limits of the province of Xalisco, all the pueblos through which

---

3. Calvo et al., *Xalisco*, 80.
4. "Nuño de Guzmán," 376, 378, 382.

the Christians passed were deserted, and they neither expected nor did there appear any Indians, except [in] a pueblo called Acatlan, where the Indians met them peacefully. And when they passed the pueblo of Xalisco, it was at war, because the people were outside the pueblo in some hills with their bows and arrows and shouting at the Christians. And they went to the pueblo of Tepic, where they found the royal inspector [Peralmindez Cherinos] and Francisco Verdugo, who had arrived there first by another road, and they said that [they] had found the said pueblo at war. Later, after Nuño de Guzmán arrived at Tepic, he sent some *nahuatatos*[5] to Xalisco to see if they would come to obedience of Your Majesty, and they did not wish to, but rather the messengers said that they had been treated badly. [Testimony of Juan Hernández Infante]

Two other Spaniards provided more explicit descriptions of the violence that occurred in Xalisco with the arrival of Guzmán's forces. One appears in chapter 2 in the account of Cristóbal Flores.[6] Pedro de Carranza's account included a horrifying episode of cruelty.

When we went to Xalisco, we found the people on the hillside where they had ascended; I do not know if it was from fear. . . . After the army lodged in Tepic, it is said that they sent for them, and in this time the Indians killed a Spaniard. It is not known if because of this they did not dare come, and it is said that he [Guzmán] sent to require them with a notary, that they should be at peace. I don't know what answer the notary brought. . . . We went up in the mountains, and from the heights they ordered that the Indians set fire and burn all the houses, which they did. Then we were all day traveling through those mountains with great effort, and he arrived at a small river and they captured two Indians, who were from there [Xalisco]. They cut off the hands of one and tied them by his skin, and his nose; they cut off the hands of the other as well, which

5. The term *nahuatato* could mean any speaker of Nahuatl, but as used by the Spanish in this period, it usually referred to an interpreter who could translate between Nahuatl and another language.

6. "Cuarta relación anónima" (credited to Cristóbal Flores), in García Icazbalceta, *Colección de documentos*, 469.

xalixco

FIGURE 5 Battle for Xalisco. Note the contrast between the more elaborate weaponry and battle garb of the Spaniards' indigenous allies compared to those of the warriors of Xalisco, one of whom uses a bow and arrow. Chavero, *Lienzo de Tlaxcala*.

also were left hanging from his skin. All this Nuño de Guzmán ordered to be done, and he told them he would do this to everyone if they did not come [to obedience].[7]

The Xalisco account describes events of the early to mid-1530s only very briefly.

Later another conqueror came, Cristóbal de Oñate. They again summoned the governors. ____ Once again they greeted

7. Razo Zaragoza, *Crónicas de la conquista,* 164. The phrase "to require them" refers to the standard declaration of the Requirement; the Indians who were responsible for the burning would have been the Indians who accompanied Guzmán from central Mexico. For the episode in which slaves were taken in Xalisco midway through Guzmán's campaign and one of its rulers was burned, see the account of Cristóbal Flores in chapter 2.

them in the same fashion, each with a jar of gold. ____ We
were conquered; many were killed in the night ____ people
asleep ____ enemies. Then he ordered that he wanted to go
to Colhuacan.[8] ____ There many commoners were all tied
with chains. ____ Don Pedro Quilt and another named Luis,
we know that perhaps they went for four years ____. They
came here and lived in Tepic. We built houses. ____ Don
Guzmán went to Mexico. Afterward ____ [a *mayordomo?*]
of Oñate came to live and later a governor who went to Yan-
cuictlalpan ____ [Vázquez] de Coronado. . . .[9]

Another fragment of the text refers to one of the Franciscan friars,
fray Pablo, who arrived with the conquerors, and the beginning of
the imposition of tribute. The next item in the account refers to an
episode that from a Spanish report that is known to have occurred
in 1537. The Spaniards pressured the leaders of Xalisco to help them
capture some people from another pueblo, Acuitlapilco. Both pueblos
were Tecuexe, but the people of Acuitlapilco lived in the mountains.
The two communities appear to have maintained some relations but
were not closely allied. The Spaniards accused the people of Acuitlapilco, whom they called Chichimecas, of committing violent acts
against other Indians.

Here first [we start] with how Domingo de Arteaga afflicted
us, and it is said that it was by the order of our lord the captain
[Oñate]. They afflicted [don] Cristóbal and the nobles and interpreters.[10] He said, listen, our lord said about the Chichimecas
that since we always kill them in the road, our lord [Oñate]
says you have to summon the people of Acuitlapilco. He wants
twenty people, not ten but exactly twenty, and if you do not
obey he will ____ greatly. Obey him, and if you do what the

8. Culiacan is the northernmost settlement established by Nuño de Guzmán in
what today is Sinaloa.

9. Calvo et al., *Xalisco*, 80.

10. The captain is Cristóbal de Oñate, the encomendero. Domingo de Arteaga was
one of his mayordomos, or stewards, and the Spaniard most closely in contact with the
pueblo in the 1530s. Nuño de Guzmán reported that Xalisco had two rulers; see Razo
Zaragoza, *Crónicas de la conquista*, 52. Both apparently received the Christian name
of Cristóbal at baptism, but one died fairly soon after the Spaniards established themselves in the area.

lord orders he will love you very much and give you _____ and all the things that you need he will give you. Quickly send your messenger there, said Domingo de Arteaga. And we said to him, listen, my lord, the people of Acuitlapilco _____ our brothers, perhaps we are not brothers with them, perhaps they are not our enemies. Whoever goes quickly there they will kill them. He answered our words angrily and said _____. And we the rulers said, in order to test the Chichimecas we will send our younger brothers,[11] who will test them, we said, and then they took all the things that would please the Chichimecas, ornaments of gold to give to them _____ and salt, all the things that they value _____ we said. Later we ordered our younger brothers. _____ Only I will summon them, so that they don't say _____ and then they said thus to the Chichimecas. And they said, it is fine, we will go there they said to him _____ and then they came. They came to speak. And Domingo [de Arteaga] our lord again said, where are the Chichimecas? We said they are still coming. Then here he began to afflict us, the captain made us miserable with the affliction regarding the Chichimecas and we became sad. We discussed how to gather the ornaments and earrings and salt so they would go there again to Acuitlapilco. When our envoy once again returned, our lord came to afflict us, me, don Cristóbal and the rulers and nobles; I fainted at their hands and so they did to us; all this was done when we already were afflicted. Then came _____ our younger brothers and said, the day after tomorrow I should expect the Chichimecas.

So we awaited them, made arrangements with those who went to satisfy them. Then eighteen came and I, don Cristóbal, made the Chichimecas content, and we sent them with Cristóbal de Oñate. Then they came to take away the Chichimecas. They took them tied by their hands to Tepic and then seized all the Chichimecas. Then he said to me that he was going to pay me, that he would give me cotton cloth and gold, and he was going to give me a horse and also anything else that the captain and Domingo, the mayordomo,[12] and a Christian named

---

11. "Our younger brothers" probably refers here to commoners of the pueblo.
12. As Oñate's mayordomo, Domingo de Arteaga kept a close watch over the community and seems to have lived in the pueblo, or nearby, much of the time.

Martín Benítez[13] mentioned to me. Before anything else they mentioned to me that it was well what you organized, and then they took them to keep them in jail. There in the jail some of the Chichimecas died from hunger and when they went to hang them they ordered us to make the ropes with which to hang them and forced us to hurry in making the ropes. Here again Domingo made us faint. _____ He greatly tormented us, me, don Cristóbal, the nobles and interpreters, he made us suffer, we were afflicted for things they made up.

When another lord came whom we did not know, he arrived there at Tepic, and perhaps at his order the Chichimecas were hanged.[14] Then we were ordered to arrange for the food and turkeys and tamales, all the kinds of food that they were going to eat there. They started on the way there, through the woods. We thought that maybe there they were going to pay us when they hanged the Chichimecas. They were hanged in front of many people: Cristóbal de Oñate, Domingo, Martín Benítez, Juan Pascual,[15] and other Christians who had gone there when they finally hanged the Chichimecas. They ate there on the road, there [where] the Chichimecas killed the people. And there we went and nothing was given to us; we lost our possessions that we gave to the Chichimecas for nothing and for nothing did we endure the work and did they cleave our head, for that reason they afflicted us [which] is all the captain and Domingo did. In this fashion we bought the Chichimecas. Twice the captain beat me, and Domingo [did] also. The fourth time they beat me, don Cristóbal, because of the Chichimecas, also the nobles and interpreters. This is all you will hear, oh lord.[16]

This episode was reported by the man who succeeded Nuño de Guzmán as governor in 1537, Lic. Diego Pérez de la Torre, as follows.

13. Martín Benítez acted as an interpreter (*lengua*); see Justicia 337, AGI.

14. This other "lord" must have been Lic. Diego Pérez de la Torre, who replaced Nuño de Guzmán as governor of Nueva Galicia in 1537.

15. Juan Pascual was a Spaniard who served as Guzmán's interpreter in Michoacan and later in Nueva Galicia.

16. Calvo et al., *Xalisco*, 81–82.

Seventeen of them were made prisoner, and their confessions [were taken] that in this period on different days they had killed many Indians on the said road, shooting them with arrows and cutting off their heads . . . and doing other very cruel things. . . . [From the jail in Compostela] they were taken to the place and crossing where they had done the said crimes and there were shot with arrows while alive and hanged, and being at the foot of the gallows eight of them were approached by a priest, the curate of the said city of Compostela, with interpreters instructing them in the matters of our Holy Faith [asking] if they wanted to be[come] Christians. . . . They said yes and they wanted to die in the faith of the Christians, and they were baptized by the said priest with a jar of water and given Christian names with their godfathers [there], and then at that moment they were hanged. After they were hanged the judge [Licenciado de la Torre] ordered them to be shot with arrows to instill more fear in the others. . . . Two others, the oldest, died in the stocks in the said city of Compostela.[17]

The account from Xalisco continues, describing how the people were forced to meet the Spaniards' tribute demands.

Here is what they made us suffer with. They afflicted the commoners when they quickly finished the maize field for tribute. Then he said, now he ordered them, the commoners, rapidly to harvest the *milpa* [cultivated field]. I will pay. So we obeyed; the commoners picked the field. Altogether four hundred commoners harvested the maize. He did not pay the commoners; Domingo de Arteaga the mayordomo just lied in what he said.

And here is how they made us suffer for the field in the dry season there in Tecomatlan. Twice we sowed the field in the dry season. He said, you make the field there in Tecomatlan . . . your work and perhaps not your purchase; do it, he said. ____ In truth, we quickly obeyed the Christian. ____ There we made the *milpa*.

17. Justicia 337, AGI.

By his authority and that of Melchor Díaz[18] ____ a house
was made that would be the house of the captain Cristóbal
de Oñate. They did not build a large house and [it was]
surrounded by stone. When it was finished then the messenger came who once again summoned all the rulers. The
Christian Melchor Díaz said you, your ruler will hand over
your ____ and fifty men and fifty women; they will look for
gold, which the lord requires, and you will not suffer. See that
now you have no other tribute. For this quickly gather your
younger brothers that they will be taking turns. . . .[19] Then
we gathered the younger brothers whom they asked for, how
many we would then hand over. ____ Here we killed them.[20]
And the Christian then wrote that we summon the captain
Cristóbal de Oñate; he then came; here he said, you should
work hard now that you will have no other tribute other than
looking for gold; every seven days they will be alternating in
order to prepare food for themselves. So said the captain. Then
they went into the woods; two months they were moving
around and nowhere did they see gold. For that reason they left
for Colhuacan [Culiacan], and we gave them things, we gave
them what they needed in the way of blankets and the women
whom they needed. . . . All the people by scores carried the food
and all went to Colhuacan. With them they counted, they were
counted altogether 50. That is all. The food was carried, altogether those who went to Colhuacan were 160. That is all that
happened.

And another time ____ the Christian who was mayordomo, named Hernando, made us work three years, 400 [loads]
of maize and 200 loads of maize and 20 of chili and 120 of
salt and 20 loads of chia that the mayordomo asked from
us ____ and Melchor Díaz. Both Christians asked for eleven
men to care for the pigs and sheep, and women, ____ three to

18. Melchor Díaz was the *alcalde* of San Miguel de Culiacan when Álvar Núñez
Cabeza de Vaca arrived there in 1536. He later participated in the expedition of
Vázquez de Coronado, crossing the Colorado River to the California side and dying as
the result of an accident in late 1540 or early 1541.
19. Encomienda labor was supposed to rotate among adult males on a regular
basis. It is clear that the Spaniards who controlled Xalisco often violated this rule.
20. "Here we killed them" probably means they sent them to their death.

prepare food, and greatly he made me, don Cristóbal, suffer for no reason because of the turkeys. _____ And he afflicted my interpreter. This is all that the Christian mayordomo Hernando did during the four years. He made all of us suffer, he afflicted the commoners. . . .[21]

[Domingo de Arteaga in particular is credited with increasing the demands on the people and resources of Xalisco.]

He [Oñate] initiated the great tribute, and another time the captain came with Domingo de Arteaga.[22] He gathered all of us rulers together and said, now listen; he ordered them to hand over their commoners, 80 men and also women, 160. You all know that I suffered much, that nothing is mine, not my cape or my horse; I will need all of it, perhaps you will give me all the gold I need and will give it in tribute, and if you do not want [to do it] for this reason, I say that the men of Guzmán will show [you how]. There is much gold here in Uitzitzillan, that everyone will go there, the 80 men and women equally that I am requesting. All those who are there in Colhuacan will come. _____ All will go together there, and maybe only I will need them, perhaps not with them; they are going to get rich when much gold appears, said the captain. Then we responded, we said, why are you asking us all this again; perhaps there are not already those who are in Colhuacan? _____ We don't accept handing over all again. He said, give me [in] all 60; again we said, it is not possible, oh lord! Again he said, it can be 40; again we said, we do not want [to], oh lord! Where will we take them from; perhaps they are nothing more than turkeys; perhaps you know that our commoners are [not?] many. We did not want [to], and he left us very angry, and later we discussed that we would hand over 20, we told him. That is all we are going to give. Twenty is all we will give you, oh lord. He said again that it should be a total of 30 men and as many women. So we again discussed it, and we handed over 60 altogether. Then we gave them gifts, to each a cotton cloak and also to the women and all the things that they needed, and then the Christian

---

21. Calvo et al., *Xalisco*, 83. Because no surname is given for this man it has not been possible to identify him.

22. Arteaga remained in Nueva Galicia. In 1559 he was a vecino of Compostela.

mayordomo Domingo left, and those we had provided went there, and they did not all arrive rapidly, and then all the rulers suffered a great deal. It was ordered that the mayordomo Domingo would make us suffer. For what reason were we treated thus? . . .

Here is the second thing that the mayordomo made us provide in tribute in making the house. The houses were large, and when we started on them, our suffering was great as we dragged the wood; it was we ourselves, the rulers, who dragged it. We did not do it with gladness but rather with suffering, and with the fence all was finished but it was not [done] with happiness. Domingo made us suffer a great deal. The second thing that Domingo made us do in tribute was the great planting for tribute that we did. He told us that all that would be produced was 6,400 loads of maize. The mayordomo Domingo kept everything, and we handed over 3,200 loads [of maize] and 150 bushels of beans, and in my house they built the millstones. The maize from us, the commoners, was 1,600 bushels; I collected it all and if not all ____. Domingo made us suffer a lot; he made us faint; he split our heads. In all 100 bushels of salt, for that we staggered ____. Salt altogether for two years we handed over 60 bushels, and 600 lengths of cotton cloth, 600 gourds also, and ____ 600 pots for carrying water altogether, ____ jars of honey, and this I always left with our señor captain in the house of the mayordomo. What I list is what in one day we gave in tribute of honey each year ____ and everything that is mentioned here they made us suffer a lot for ____ if we were missing a little of the tribute. They did not take care of us.

And here. What we here put, what we gave in tribute during Lent: 10 loads of big haddock, 10 loads of prawns and ____ loads of oysters; every twenty days all was delivered. Also when Lent ended in total: 10 loads of big haddock, 10 loads of prawns and 6 loads of oysters. All this we had to provide each Lent, and with all this we suffered and lost a great deal ____ in order to buy fish because the fishermen do not catch them. As for eggs during Lent, they were 2,000. . . . When Lent ended we delivered 35 (?) [sic] turkeys and 80 rabbits and innumerable quails, 200 ducks and innumerable *mojarras* [sea bream] ____ and 300 Spanish chickens, and the rabbits, quails, and ducks. In two Lenten seasons twice we gave tribute, not always; only in two years did we provide tribute, and all these things that are mentioned always were given each Lent. It was asked of us, and if we did not hand over everything ____.

Here we explain what we suffered in the above-mentioned tribute with what they made us suffer; with each kind of tribute they made us suffer. They made us faint; they cleaved our heads, even if it would be [only] by a little that we lacked in tribute, even if it were a tiny amount, for this we worked too much that they made us faint, and we went around fearful and worried; at no moment were we happy. For this reason we lost much of our possessions, our gold, our turquoise, our cotton blankets; for this we lost and we, the rulers, felt anguish. We paid it ourselves, not with the property of the commoners but with the gold of those of us who governed: I, don Cristóbal, don Juan de Oñate, don Pedro, don Diego, don Francisco, don Alonso, don Juan, don Rodrigo, don Gonzalo, don Francisco, we all suffered a lot and lost our possessions because of the tribute. And we ____. For this reason they made us suffer; they split all of our heads: I, Francisco, Melchor, Alonso, Juan, and although all of this we suffered, we did not for that reason commit wrongs; we were not envious, [unlike] others who committed wrongs and became like Chichimecas (rebelling), although we lost much of our possessions to buy what Cristóbal de Oñate needed. . . .[23]

[The account mentions another Spaniard, Francisco Cornejo, who also oversaw the collection of tribute and required at least six women to work at grinding corn every week.[24]]

Here is what was provided in tribute to the house of the mayordomo Domingo. Everything that was provided in tribute was five loads of firewood a day, and eighty tamales a day were provided, and two turkeys delivered daily, and a gourd of salt

23. Calvo et al., *Xalisco*, 84–86.
24. Cornejo was born in 1512 and arrived in Mexico shortly before joining Guzmán's entrada. He claimed to have gone to New Mexico but also to have participated in the suppressing the Mixton rebellion, so perhaps he returned early from New Mexico. In the late 1550s he was living in Guadalajara. One of his sons became a priest and could speak Nahuatl.

every day, and a gourd of chili. And it fell to me, don Cristóbal, to me alone to deliver eggs on Fridays, and my turkeys they always took; sometimes they took seven of my turkeys and sometimes ten. We were three: I, don Cristóbal; and my assistants; I, Francisco; and I ____. It is known that he took turkeys from Martinico and Juan. . . . They afflicted us and mistreated us and not everything that was made in tribute arrived in the house of Domingo Arteaga, and they greatly scolded and mistreated the boys. . . . [25]

Here is something else that Domingo made us do in tribute. ____ He said to us: Now make a large field of cotton so from here will be produced cotton cloth that your younger brothers who are washing gold need, and soon those who are in Colhuacan will arrive, because they are going to be here together, there where they wash gold. For this reason you will prepare the field of cotton. In all we harvested 120 large loads and then everything was kept in the house of Domingo, the mayordomo. Everything was put there, and he gave us, it was delivered to us, 200 lengths of cotton cloth, each one a *braza* and a half [wide] and the same in length, and if we had not made them that way he would have split our heads; he mistreated us. And before all of us, the rulers, they counted the cotton and the total number of mantas was 600.

Here is another thing. They, the washers of gold who lived there in Colhuacan, they were washing gold for three years, and when they came here to our home not all came; a total of twenty-five men died. And the women who went to die, thirty-two did not return. . . . [26]

[The account provides more detail about the cultivation of cotton. The mayordomo Domingo de Arteaga forced the pueblo to buy land in Tecomatlan to raise cotton. The ruling group, together with several of their interpreters and "three who were not yet baptized," used their own cotton cloth for the purchase. They harvested 250 loads of cotton from the field in the first

---

25. Calvo et al., *Xalisco*, 87. When Hernando Cortés passed through the area in 1535 en route to Baja California, Oñate made the people of Xalisco provide supplies for him and his party as well.

26. Ibid., 88.

year. After several years they did not want to continue because of the hot climate.]

Because we did not want to go there he mistreated us, the lords. And because of their mistreatment of us and of all our commoners, we ordered them that no one should stay. Then we went to work on the cotton field there in Tecomatlan. And there many were lost; they became ill because they were unaccustomed to the heat, because there it is very hot. And we suffered along with them, all of us, six altogether, who were working there got sick: don Francisco, don Pedro, don Juan Dionicio, don Francisco, and ____; the lords who were in the six places and the commoners all began to get sick. In all, we counted 240 men together with the lords ____. And it did not yield much [cotton], and in vain we got sick [and] died. Only 20 loads were produced. . . .

Here is another thing that Domingo de Arteaga forced us to provide in tribute, when our master the captain and all the Christians in Compostela wanted to build a house. So once again we built his house, very large, and we and the women were carrying mud and adobe bricks. Those who hauled did not rest. When the house was built, we did not do it with pleasure, for this Domingo made us suffer greatly. We built the house twice and only when it was finished did we all rest. . . .[27]

[The people working in Culiacan washing gold continued to die, and the Spaniards demanded replacements. Some of the people tried to escape, at one time a dozen, which resulted in the punishment of the pueblo's rulers and demands that the escapees be rounded up or replaced. They were coerced into handing over another ten men and some women as well.]

Here is the other way that the mayordomo Domingo made us suffer; he made up ways and for no reason he made us suffer. We nobles, we do not know for what reason he treated us so, for reasons we do not know, he made us faint in the house of Melchor, the interpreter. We were tortured on a wooden beam, and one person ____. Our ruler don Cristóbal, he made

27. Calvo et al., *Xalisco*, 90–91. Guzmán chose Compostela as the capital of Nueva Galicia, as it was in a heavily populated area near the substantial indigenous community of Tepic.

him suffer separately, and because of this he got sick and died. And when we were handed over we were told that it was because we were bad and did not obey. Perhaps they will turn into Chichimecas. The mayordomo Domingo always spoke to us angrily. . . .[28]

Here is something else about when a governor arrived here whom we did not know, and Captain Cristóbal de Oñate, our master, came and another captain, Juan de Villalba, and the mayordomo Domingo de Arteaga, and we did not know that he came on our behalf, to help us with what we suffered.[29] And when we met him, the Captain Cristóbal de Oñate had us assemble, with Juan de Villalba and the mayordomo Domingo and also we three, I, don Cristóbal; I, don Rodrigo; and our interpreter Alonso. We were all summoned in secret. Said the captain, now, what do you say, the governor who came here perhaps is going to question you about how are afflicted, and you know that your mayordomo, Domingo, here loves you very much. You should not go to him with anything, something with which the mayordomo might afflict you. I will punish [you] if you show anything to the governor, who soon will leave. And they did not say anything. Perhaps you will give him something to eat; if you do not say anything to him, I will love you; I will give you mantas every year and oxen with which to plow. To you, don Cristóbal, I will give two different kinds of cows and to the nobles one kind. And also to you, the interpreter, you will get one kind. And I will give you instruments; I will give you gold; I will give you [things] because he always has made you suffer; these are the things I will give. And we answered him, it is good, oh, our lord. Let it be so that you will show favor to the señores, your vassals, so it will be; we will not denounce [you], we told him. And then we met so as to have just one version [to present] before the governor.

28. Calvo et al., *Xalisco*, 93. There had been two rulers in Xalisco named don Cristóbal.

29. The "governor" who arrived almost certainly was one of the judges of the audiencia in Mexico City, Lic. Lorenzo de Tejada, who visited Nueva Galicia in 1545 as part of an effort to introduce the New Laws. These laws, among other things, were intended to limit the rights of encomenderos to indigenous labor and personal service. Tejada is mentioned by name later in the account.

Then the next day he summoned us. He asked each, he said, are you happy here in your home, that your lord does not make you suffer, or his mayordomo does not make you suffer. Tell me; do not be afraid. I came to help you. I came for you, the lord said. And we said to him, you have shown us favor, lord. Why would we denounce him if he loves us well, never did he mistreat us, we said. And only because we were commanded did we speak thus, and if we had not been ordered, we truly would have communicated to the governor how we were mistreated. We thought that we would be given all the things that our master had mentioned. They were inventions. The mayordomo Domingo falsely kissed and swore before the lord with which he lied, and he did not reveal how he made us suffer. The captain said that never in all time will I and the mayordomo Domingo mistreat them.

And he said he never would mistreat us. And it was too much what they had done and how much they made us suffer. And to me, don Rodrigo, he told me that if I denounced anything, I will kill you in secret. And now we declare how much Domingo made us suffer. And when our beloved fathers, the guardian fray Fernando and fray Francisco de Pastrana, came to save our soul, they established for ten years the field of cacao in Santa Cruz.[30]

As suggested by the failure of Lorenzo de Tejada's visit to change conditions in Xalisco, the people of the pueblo continued to suffer exploitation and abuse at the hands of the Spaniards. After the unsuccessful attempt to raise cotton in Tecomatlan, the Spaniards hoped to find a more viable and lucrative crop in cacao, mentioned earlier. Cacao was a highly valued commodity in Mesoamerica, both as the basis for a drink and for use as currency. The Xalisco account continues.

Oh our lord, another thing that we want to tell, we want you to know that at a certain moment this began in this fashion. They assembled us, all the lords, the nobles, the overseers [*tequitlatos*, from Nahuatl], and the interpreter Alonso Miciu. ____ Our

30. Calvo et al., *Xalisco*, 94–95.

captain, Cristóbal de Oñate, assembled us, he said, now listen, you lords. Here I want you to begin to cultivate the field of cacao there in Santa Cruz. Because something else is suffering, sowing cacao is very good; it produces a lot; you will be very happy, all the lords and their commoners. All those who are in the gold placers will leave; all will be together there in the clearing in Santa Cruz; no longer will they be in the gold placers, [as] this will be all of your tribute. Only if it produces well, all your other work will disappear; you will be very happy, when it produces well you will become rich ____ as soon as it produces cacao, and to each lord will be given eight thousand seeds and to the overseers also it will be given, and the commoners also will be given cacao; you will drink it; it will not be scarce ____. For this truly you will be happy. All this Cristóbal de Oñate said, all before the Christians named Alonso de Roa and Alonso Liquis and the mayordomo Domingo de Arteaga. Then we answered him, listen, oh our lord, you know well it is your favor. All the people who died and perhaps again many men will die; they will get sick and die; perhaps it is not possible. We do not need it and it is very hot there, we said. He said, you will not do it in Tecomatlan but in Santa Cruz, nearby. . . .

Then we said, perhaps it will be given to us. We will prepare the field of cacao; perhaps only those who now are in the gold mines will be occupied in doing it, and perhaps they truly will give each of us eight thousand cacao seeds. . . . Happily, we met and in this way we talked to our commoners about all the things that our lord the captain mentioned, and for this reason the commoners also became happy. Then we went with the captain there to Santa Cruz, all of us rulers taking with us our commoners; we took altogether two hundred. We cut trees; we dug the earth. We were there on a Sunday. . . .

[Initially, Oñate seems to have promised that the people of Santa Cruz would do most of the labor, but that turned out not to be the case. Instead, the people of Xalisco, men and women, found themselves responsible for the hard and probably unfamiliar work of planting and maintaining the trees.]

Another time the mayordomo Domingo said, you will go there again to Santa Cruz; to the cacao orchard you will go to plant the trees. And all the women dragged the trees. And Domingo took many commoners to plant the trees. . . . And another time Domingo said, now you, the nobles and lords, will leave your sons so they can go to the cacao orchard. They will return; they will return as soon as they have finished their work. Ten men are needed and three women to prepare their food, Domingo said. And then began all ten men and the three women, and it was not certain when they would return. They were there a year and a half; they paid them nothing. They returned sadly. And we, the lords, then were there a year and a half. This is not work for us, but at that time señor Tejada was not still there, and many times we went back to Santa Cruz. We took many commoners with their women. And a Christian cacao grower named Andrés Pérez was established there, there he began to split our heads of us nobles and don Cristóbal. He made us endure the work along with our commoners. He made us endure too much work; he mistreated us; he made us dispirited as if we were dogs, and that work was not suitable for us.

I, don Cristóbal, truly I do not lie, in the four times I went, the first time I went I took 200 commoners, and he, the Christian Andrés Pérez, made two persons suffer. He opened the head of one; he split it open. He struck another person on the neck with his sword and made him faint. When he became conscious again, he tied him to a pole for the whole day. The second time I went, I took 400 commoners, along with all their lords. The third time that I, don Cristóbal, went I took 120 commoners. The fourth time I took 60 commoners altogether. That is what I, don Cristóbal, know.

Another time I, Rodrigo, went as supervisor, and all of us nobles, no one remained, and many of the commoners, altogether 500 commoners, went, and he made them suffer. . . . Every day Andrés Pérez made us suffer a great deal; at times he split our heads; sometimes he had the dogs bite them; sometimes at his hands they fainted; at his hands they died. So it went and it was not our work; we worked for nothing; they did not pay us; it was not what we had been ordered. . . .[31]

31. Ibid., 95–97.

Domingo de Arteaga ignored Lorenzo de Tejada's stipulation that he not live in Xalisco and continued to demand that women come to prepare his food and work in his household. When two women fled from Arteaga's service, Alonso de Roa went at night to the homes of don Cristóbal and don Rodrigo and beat them. Arteaga also demanded that the rulers of the pueblo provide boys to irrigate the cacao orchards. The illegal demands and abuses continued unchanged, and people working in Santa Cruz sickened and died. The Spaniards tried cultivating cacao in Tecomatlan as well. There too workers were beaten and in other ways mistreated.

> At their hands many collapsed there and then died. Some we brought back; some died in the road; some died in the woods; some came back to their houses to die; others came here to die; in total 123 of our children died.[32]

Perhaps surprisingly, the account from Xalisco does not include any mention of the great rebellion of 1540–42. Testimony that was taken from Xalisco's long-suffering ruler, don Cristóbal, reflects his experiences during the war. At the time that he testified, he was about thirty years old and a baptized Christian.[33]

> It was well known to this witness, and some of his Indians made him aware from other Indian singers of the rebellion and uprising and devil's chant [tlatol] that was going around and started among the Zacatecas and Cazcanes, of whom this witness learned from many Indians were going around as messengers through many of the pueblos of this province of Nueva Galicia. . . . This witness sent some of his Indians to other pueblos that he regarded as friendly to find out and [make them] understand that everything that those Cazcan and Zacateca Indians were saying was . . . lies, and he did this two or three times. And this witness's messengers told him that the pueblos of his friends like Tetitlan and Iztlan did not want to do what he advised. He once again sent a messenger, a noble of his pueblo, and not only were

---

32. Ibid., 103. There were major epidemics that affected much of the region in the mid to late 1540s that probably contributed to the growing mortality.

33. Justicia 262, AGI.

they unwilling and did not want to do what he advised, but they killed the said messenger, whom he believes they killed in the pueblo of Tetitlan. And the Cazcan and Zacateca Indians sent to this witness to say, via the Indians of Xalisco whom he had sent as messengers, whom they told this, that they should abandon their faith and the beliefs of the Christians and return to theirs of the devil, and they knew and held as certain that they would kill all the Christians with the help and favor of their great devil, who had made a great opening in the earth where the Christians would go. And that there would come a great fire sent by the devil and would burn all the Christians and the Indians who did not want to rebel. Then they would go on to Mexico, which they would subdue, and they would do the same there.

Although we can only speculate how much of this testimony was supplied by the Spaniards who conducted the inquiry and how much don Cristóbal provided of his own accord, don Cristóbal's subsequent testimony suggests that it resulted from the same kind of pressure that Oñate and Arteaga exerted to persuade the rulers of Xalisco not to say anything negative when Licenciado Tejada visited the pueblo in the mid-1540s after the war.

This witness [don Cristóbal] always was well treated and never saw nor found out that any Indians of this province were mistreated by their masters or by other Christians because if they had they would have risen up but rather the said uprising was caused by the chant of the devil, as he has said.

The ruling group in Xalisco struggled to meet the unrelenting demands of their encomendero and his retainers and to maintain the community's neutrality during the Mixton War. During the 1530s and 1540s don Cristóbal and the other principal men of the pueblo found themselves in the impossible position of trying to satisfy the Spaniards and provide some protection for the commoners—their "little brothers"—while attempting to maintain their own rapidly diminishing wealth. Forced into complicity with the Spaniards, as in the episode in which they used their own possessions to lure the "Chichimecas" of Acuitlapilco into the Spaniards' hands, they gained nothing from acting as unwilling intermediaries.

This volume begins with Tenamaztle's bitter denunciation of the Spanish regime and ends with a portrait of Spanish exploitation and abuse of a once-prosperous community of the west. Although in retrospect the outcome of the clash between Spanish ambitions and indigenous resistance in Nueva Galicia may seem a foregone conclusion, that inevitability should not obscure what their hard-fought struggle meant for the peoples of the west. The accounts included here are intended to illuminate that struggle and its consequences.

TIMELINE FOR THE HISTORY OF EARLY NUEVA GALICIA

1524	Francisco Cortés leads entrada north from Colima
1525	Visit of communities contacted by Cortés conducted
1527	Nuño de Guzmán arrives in New Spain as governor of Pánuco
1528	Guzmán is appointed president of the first audiencia of Mexico
May 1529	Audiencia authorizes Guzmán's expedition to the west
Dec. 1529	Guzmán departs Mexico City for Michoacan and the entrada to the west
Feb. 1530	Expedition departs Michoacan; execution of the cazonci
July 1530	Guzmán writes letter to the king from Omitlan on the Pacific coast
Sept. 1530	Hurricane and flood cause huge mortality and damage at Aztatlan
Jan. 1531	Guzmán's expedition departs Chiametla for the north
April 1531	Expedition reaches Culiacan
1531	Founding of San Miguel de Culicacan, Compostela, and Guadalajara
1535–36	Guzmán authorizes and carries out slaving campaigns in Nueva Galicia
April 1535	Don Antonio de Mendoza is appointed first viceroy of New Spain
March 1536	Lic. Diego Pérez de la Torre arrives in New Spain, appointed as new governor of Nueva Galicia
Spring 1536	Álvar Núñez Cabeza de Vaca's party reaches Culiacan
June 1536	Cabeza de Vaca's party arrives in Compostela and is received by Guzmán
Late 1536	Guzmán travels to Mexico City to greet the viceroy
Jan. 1537	Guzmán is arrested and jailed in Mexico City
April 1537	Licenciado Pérez de la Torre arrives in Nueva Galicia
Late 1538	Francisco Vázquez de Coronado arrives in Nueva Galicia as new governor
Feb. 1540	Vázquez de Coronado departs from Compostela with expedition to New Mexico
Mid-1540	The indigenous uprising begins in Nueva Galicia

Nov. 1540	Pedro de Alvarado meets with Mendoza in Michoacan and agrees to become a partner in the exploration of the South Sea
Dec. 1540	Mendoza arrives in port of Navidad on the Pacific coast
March 1541	Miguel de Ibarra and Franciscans go to Juchipila and try unsuccessfully to persuade the Indians to submit; Mendoza meets with local officials, Franciscans, and others to deliberate on a course of action
April 1541	Cristóbal de Oñate and his forces are defeated after besieging Mixton
June 1541	Reinforcements from the South Sea fleet arrive in Guadalajara and other places; Juan de Alvarado brings Spanish and indigenous troops from Michoacan
Late June 1541	Pedro de Alvarado attacks Nochistlan and in early July and dies of injuries received during the retreat
Summer 1541	The indigenous rebellion spreads
Sept. 1541	The siege of Guadalajara is broken
Oct. 1541	Mendoza arrives at Coyna leading a large Spanish and indigenous army
Dec. 1541	Fall of the peñol of Mixton
March 1542	The Mixton War ends
1546	Pedro Gómez de Maraver is appointed the first bishop of Nueva Galicia
Late 1546	Discovery of Zacatecas mines
1548	Establishment of the first audiencia of Nueva Galicia
1552	Mendoza leaves New Spain for Peru; don Luis de Velasco becomes the second viceroy
	Tenamaztle, former lord of Nochistlan, Christian convert, and rebel leader, is sent into exile in Spain

GLOSSARY

adelantado	leader granted civil and judicial powers by the Spanish Crown
ají	chili peppers
alcalde mayor	district governor
alcalde ordinario	magistrate of the first instance
arroba	weight of approximately twenty-five pounds
audiencia	high court
braza	linear measure of approximately two yards
cabildo	municipal council
cacica	female ruler
cacique	indigenous ruler
cazonci	Purépecha (Tarascan) ruler
Chichimecas	generic term used by Spaniards for independent Indians considered to be uncivilized
corregidor	governor, district administrator
criado	servant or retainer
cue	temple
ducados	ducats, approximately 400 maravedís
encomendero	holder of an encomienda
encomienda	grant of right to extract tribute and labor from a specific group of Indians
entrada	expedition of reconnaissance or conquest
indios amigos	Indian allies or friendly Indians
información	deposition
lengua	interpreter (literally, tongue)
licenciado	holder of an advanced university degree
macana	wooden sword edged with obsidian
manta	indigenous cotton cloth
mayordomo	steward, manager
milpa	cultivated field
mitote	dance
mojarra	sea bream
naboría	servant, auxiliary
nahuatato	interpreter, Nahuatl speaker (from Nahuatl, *nahuatlato*)
oidor	audiencia judge

peñol	mountainous, fortified stronghold
principal	Spanish term for an indigenous noble
regidor	town councilman
repartimiento	in this period, term used interchangeably with *enco-mienda*; also any allotment or distribution of indigenous labor
residencia	investigation into an official's conduct in office
señor	lord, master
tameme	porter (from Nahuatl, *tlameme*)
tequitlato	overseer (from Nahuatl)
teul	strong, powerful being (from Nahuatl, *teotl*)
tlatol	statement or chant (from Nahuatl, *tlatolli*)
vecindad	citizenship
vecino	citizen, head of household, resident, neighbor
veedor	inspector
visitación	visit of inspection

BIBLIOGRAPHY

Archival Sources

Archivo General de Indias, Seville (AGI)
    Audiencia de Mexico
    Justicia
    Mapas y Planas
Archivo General de la Nación, Mexico City (AGN)
    Hospital de Jesús
Archivo Histórico Nacional, Madrid (AHN)
    Diversos Colecciones

Published Sources and Secondary Works

Adorno, Rolena, and Patrick Charles Pautz. *Álvar Núñez Cabeza de Vaca: His Account, His Life, and the Expedition of Pánfilo de Narváez.* 3 vols. Lincoln: University of Nebraska Press, 1999.

Aiton, Arthur Scott. *Antonio de Mendoza: First Viceroy of New Spain.* New York: Russell and Russell, 1927.

Altman, Ida. "Conquest, Conversion and Collaboration: Indian Allies and the Campaigns in Nueva Galicia." In Matthew and Oudijk, *Indian Conquistadors*, 145–74.

———. "Spanish Society in Mexico City After the Conquest." *Hispanic American Historical Review* 71, no. 3 (1991): 412–45.

———. *The War for Mexico's West: Indians and Spaniards in New Galicia, 1524–1550.* Albuquerque: University of New Mexico Press, 2010.

Amaya, Jesús. *Los conquistadores Fernández de Hijar y Bracamonte.* Guadalajara: Gráfica Editorial, 1952.

Bakewell, Peter J. *Silver Mining and Society in Colonial Mexico: Zacatecas, 1546–1700.* Cambridge: Cambridge University Press, 1971.

Baus de Czitrom, Carolyn. *Tecuexes y cocas: Dos grupos de la región Jalisco en el siglo XVI.* Colección Científica 112. Serie Etnohistoria. Mexico City: INAH, 1982.

Blázquez, Adrián, and Thomas Calvo. *Guadalajara y el nuevo mundo: Nuño Beltrán de Guzmán; Semblanza de un conquistador.* Guadalajara: Institución Provincial de Cultura, 1992.

Calvo, Thomas. *La Nueva Galicia en los siglos XVI y XVII.* Zapopan: El Colegio de Jalisco, 1989.

Calvo, Thomas, Eustaquio Celestino, Magdalena Gómez, Jean Meyer, and Ricardo Xochitemol. *Xalisco, la voz de un pueblo en el siglo XVI.* Mexico City: CIESAS–CEMCA, 1993.

Chavero, Alfredo. *El Lienzo de Tlaxcala.* 1892. Facsimile, Mexico City: Cosmos, 1979.

Chipman, Donald E. *Nuño de Guzmán and the Province of Pánuco in New Spain, 1518–1533.* Glendale, Calif.: Clark, 1967.

Cuatro crónicas de la conquista del reino de Nueva Galicia. Guadalajara: Instituto Jalisciense de Antropología e Historia, 1960.

Flint, Richard. *Great Cruelties Have Been Reported: The 1544 Investigation of the Coronado Expedition.* Dallas: Southern Methodist University Press, 2002.

Foster, Michael S., and Phil C. Weigand, eds. *The Archaeology of West and Northwest Mesoamerica.* Boulder: Westview Press, 1985.

Fuentes, Patricia de, ed. and trans. *The Conquistadors: First-Person Accounts of the Conquest of Mexico.* Norman: University of Oklahoma Press, 1993.

García Icazbalceta, Joaquín. *Colección de documentos para la historia de Mexico.* Vol. 2. Mexico City: Editorial Porrua, 1971. Originally published 1858–66.

García Loaeza, Pablo, and Victoria L. Garrett, eds. *The Improbable Conquest: Sixteenth-Century Letters from the Río de la Plata.* University Park: Penn State University Press, 2015.

Gerhard, Peter. *The North Frontier of New Spain.* Rev. ed. Princeton: Princeton University Press, 1993.

Hassig, Ross. *Aztec Warfare: Imperial Expansion and Political Control.* Norman: University of Oklahoma Press, 1988.

Hillerkuss, Thomas, comp. *Documentalía del sur de Jalisco: Siglo XVI.* Zapopan: El Colegio de Jalisco; Mexico City: INAH, 1994.

Himmerich y Valencia, Robert. *The Encomenderos of New Spain, 1521–1555.* Austin: University of Texas Press, 1991.

León-Portilla, Miguel. *La flecha en el blanco: Francisco Tenamaztle y Bartolomé de las Casas en lucha por los derechos de los indígenas, 1541–1556.* Mexico City: Editorial Diana; Zapopan: El Colegio de Jalisco, 1995.

Martínez Baracs, Rodrigo. *Convivencia y utopia: El gobierno indio y español de la "Ciudad de Mechuacan," 1521–1580.* Mexico City: INAH/Fondo de Cultura Económica, 2005.

Matthew, Laura E., and Michel R. Oudijk, eds. *Indian Conquistadors: Indigenous Allies in the Conquest of Mesoamerica.* Norman: University of Oklahoma Press, 2007.

Miranda, José. "La función económica del encomendero en los orígenes del régimen colonial de Nueva España (1525–1531)." *Anales del Instituto Nacional de Antropología e Historia* 2 (1941–46): 421–62.

Muriá, José María, dir. *Historia de Jalisco*. Vol. 1, *Desde los tiempos prehistóricos hasta fines del siglo XVII*. Guadalajara: Gobierno del Estado de Jalisco, 1980.

"Nuño de Guzmán contra Hernán Cortés, sobre los descubrimientos y conquistas en Jalisco y Tepic, 1531." *Boletín del Archivo General de la Nación* 8, no. 4 (1937): 365–400, 541–76.

Orozco y Jiménez, Francisco. *Colección de documentos históricos inéditos y muy raros, referentes al arzobispado de Guadalajara*. 5 vols. Guadalajara: Trimentral Ilustrada, 1922–26.

Parry, J. H. *The Audiencia of New Galicia in the Sixteenth Century: A Study in Spanish Colonial Government*. Cambridge: Cambridge University Press, 1948.

Pérez Bustamante, Ciriaco. *Los orígenes del gobierno virreinal en las Indias españolas, don Antonio de Mendoza, primer virrey de la Nueva España, 1535–1550*. Santiago: Universidad de Santiago, 1928.

Pérez-Rocha, Emma, and Rafael Tena. *La nobleza indígena del centro de México después de la conquista*. Mexico City: INAH, 2000.

Pollard, Helen Perlstein. "Recent Research in West Mexican Archaeology." *Journal of Archaeological Research* 4 (1997): 345–82.

Powell, Philip Wayne. *Soldiers, Indians, and Silver: North America's First Frontier War*. Berkeley: University of California Press, 1952. Reprint, Tempe: Arizona State University Center for Latin American Studies, 1975.

Razo Zaragoza, José Luis, comp. *Crónicas de la conquista del reino de Nueva Galicia*. Guadalajara: Instituto Jalisciense de Antropología e Historia, 1963.

Reséndez, Andrés. *A Land So Strange: The Epic Journey of Cabeza de Vaca*. New York: Basic Books, 2007.

Restall, Matthew. *Seven Myths of the Spanish Conquest*. Oxford: Oxford University Press, 2003.

Restall, Matthew, and Florine Asselbergs. *Invading Guatemala: Spanish, Nahua, and Maya Accounts of the Conquest Wars*. University Park: Penn State University Press, 2007.

Román Gutiérrez, José Francisco. *Sociedad y evangelización en Nueva Galicia durante el siglo XVI*. Zapopan: El Colegio de Jalisco; Mexico City: INAH; Zacatecas: Universidad Autónoma de Zacatecas, 1993.

Romero de Solís, José Miguel. *El conquistador Francisco Cortés: Reivindicación de un Cobarde*. Colima: Archivo Histórico del Municipio de Colima, 1994.

Ruiz Medrano, Ethelia. *Reshaping New Spain: Government and Private Interests in the Colonial Bureaucracy, 1531–1550*. Boulder: University Press of Colorado, 2006.

Sandoval Acacictli, Francisco de. *Conquista y pacificación de los indios chichimecas*. Edited by José Maria Muriá. 2nd ed. Zapopan: El Colegio de Jalisco, 1996.

Sauer, Carl O. *Colima of New Spain in the Sixteenth Century*. 1948. Reprint, Westport, Conn.: Greenwood Press, 1976.

Schroeder, Susan. *Chimalpahin and the Kingdoms of Chalco*. Tucson: University of Arizona Press, 1991.

Schwartz, Stuart B., ed. *Victors and Vanquished: Spanish and Nahua Views of the Conquest of Mexico*. New York: Bedford/St. Martin's Press, 2000.

Tello, Antonio. *Crónica miscelánea de la Sancta Provincia de Xalisco: Libro Segundo*. Vol. 1. Guadalajara: Gobierno del Estado de Jalisco, Universidad de Guadalajara, IJAH, INAH; Jalisco: Biblioteca "José Parres Aria," 1968–87.

Warren, J. Benedict. *The Conquest of Michoacán: The Spanish Domination of the Tarascan Kingdom in Western Mexico, 1521–1530*. Norman: University of Oklahoma Press, 1985.

Weigand, Phil C., and Acelia García de Weigand. *Los orígenes de los caxcanes y su relación con la guerra de los nayaritas: Una hipótesis*. Zapopan: El Colegio de Jalisco, 1995.

———. *Tenamaxtli y Guaxicar: Las raíces profundas de la Rebelión de Nueva Galicia*. Zamora: El Colegio de Michoacán; Guadalajara: Secretaría de Cultural de Jalisco, 1996.

Williams, Eduardo, ed. *Contribuciones a la arqueología y etnohistoria del Occidente de México*. Zamora: El Colegio de Michoacán, 1994.

latin american originals

Titles in Print

Typeset by
CLICK! PUBLISHING SERVICES

Printed and bound by
SHERIDAN BOOKS

Composed in
ALDUS AND CRONOS

Printed on
NATURES NATURAL

Made in the USA
Las Vegas, NV
18 February 2023

67761022R00090